ECLECTIC SCHOOL READINGS

STORIES FROM LIFE

ORISON SWETT MARDEN

Pharos Books

ISBN: 978-93-95229-64-7
eISBN: 978-93-95229-65-4

Publisher: Pharos Books (P) Ltd.
Plot No.-55, Main Mother Dairy Road
Pandav Nagar, East Delhi-110092
Phone: 011-40395855, +14049995474
WhatsApp: +91 8368220032
E-mail: sales@pharosbooks.in
Website: www.pharosbooks.in
First Edition: 2023

Printed By: Sushma Book Binding House, Okhla
Industrial Area, Phase I, New Delhi-110020

Eclectic School Readings : Stories From Life
ORISON SWETT MARDEN

Contents

PREFACE

To make a life, as well as to make a living, is one of the supreme objects for which we must all struggle. The sooner we realize what this means, the greater and more worthy will be the life which we shall make.

In putting together the brief life stories and incidents from great lives which make up the pages of this little volume, the writer's object has been to show young people that, no matter how humble their birth or circumstances, they may make lives that will be held up as examples to future generations, even as these stories show how boys, handicapped by poverty and the most discouraging surroundings, yet succeeded so that they are held up as models to the boys of to-day.

No boy or girl can learn too early in life the value of time and the opportunities within reach of the humblest children of the twentieth century to enable them to make of themselves noble men and women.

The stories here presented do not claim to be more than mere outlines of the subjects chosen, enough to show what brave souls in the past, souls animated by loyalty to God and to their best selves, were able to accomplish in spite of obstacles of which the more fortunately born youths of to-day can have no conception.

It should never be forgotten, however, in the strivings of ambition, that, while every one should endeavor to raise himself to his highest power and to attain to as exalted and honorable a position as his abilities entitle him to, his first object should be to make a noble life.

The author wishes to acknowledge the assistance of Miss Margaret Connolly in the preparation of this volume.

O.S.M.

STORIES FROM LIFE

TO-DAY

For the structure that we raise,
    Time is with materials filled;
Our to-days and yesterdays
    Are the blocks with which we build.

LONGFELLOW.

To-day! To-day! It is ours, with all its magic possibilities of being and doing. Yesterday, with its mistakes, misdeeds, lost opportunities, and failures, is gone forever. With the morrow we are not immediately concerned. It is but a promise yet to be fulfilled. Hidden behind the veil of the future, it may dimly beckon us, but it is yet a shadowy, unsubstantial vision, one that we, perhaps, never may realize. But to-day, the Here, the Now, that dawned upon us with the first hour of the morn, is a reality, a precious possession upon the right use of which may depend all our future of happiness and success, or of misery and failure; for

"This day we fashion Destiny, our web of Fate we spin."

Lest he should forget that Time's wings are swift and noiseless, and so rapidly bear our to-days to the Land of Yesterday, John Ruskin, philosopher, philanthropist, and tireless worker though he was, kept constantly before his eyes on his study table a large, handsome block of chalcedony, on which was graven the single word "To-day." Every moment of this noble life was enriched by the right use of each passing moment.

A successful merchant, whose name is well-known throughout our country, very tersely sums up the means by which true success may be attained. “It is just this,” he says: “Do your best every day, whatever you have in hand.”

This simple rule, if followed in sunshine and in storm, in days of sadness as well as days of gladness, will rear for the builder a Palace Beautiful more precious than pearls of great price, more enduring than time.

***

"THE MILL BOY OF THE SLASHES"

A picturesque, as well as pathetic figure, was Henry Clay, the little "Mill Boy of the Slashes," as he rode along on the old family horse to Mrs. Darricott's mill. Blue-eyed, rosy-cheeked, and bare-footed, clothed in coarse shirt and trousers, and a time-worn straw hat, he sat erect on the bare back of the horse, holding, with firm hand, the rope which did duty as a bridle. In front of him lay the precious sack, containing the grist which was to be ground into meal or flour, to feed the hungry mouths of the seven little boys and girls who, with the widowed mother, made up the Clay family.

It required a good deal of grist to feed so large a family, especially when hoecake was the staple food, and it was because of his frequent trips to the mill, across the swampy region called the "Slashes," that Henry was dubbed by the neighbors "The Mill Boy of the Slashes."

The lad was ambitious, however, and, very early in life, made up his mind that he would win for himself a more imposing title. He never dreamed of winning world-wide renown as an orator, or of exchanging his boyish sobriquet for "The Orator of Ashland." But he who forms high ideals in youth usually far outstrips his first ambition, and Henry had "hitched his wagon to a star."

This awkward country boy, who was so bashful, and so lacking in self-confidence that he hardly dared recite before his class in the log schoolhouse, DETERMINED TO BECOME AN ORATOR.

Henry Clay, the brilliant lawyer and statesman, the American Demosthenes who could sway multitudes by his matchless oratory, once said, "In order to succeed a man must have a purpose fixed, then let his motto be VICTORY OR DEATH." When Henry Clay, the poor country boy, son of an unknown Baptist minister, made up his mind to become an orator, he acted on this principle. No discouragement or obstacle was allowed to swerve him from his purpose. Since the death of his father, when the boy was but five years old, he had carried grist to the mill, chopped wood, followed the plow barefooted, clerked in a country store,—did everything that a loving son and brother could do to help win a subsistence for the family.

In the midst of poverty, hard work, and the most pitilessly unfavorable conditions, the youth clung to his resolve. He learned what he could at the country schoolhouse, during the time the duties of the farm permitted him to attend school. He committed speeches to memory, and recited them aloud, sometimes in the forest, sometimes while working in the cornfield, and frequently in a barn with a horse and an ox for his audience.

In his fifteenth year he left the grocery store where he had been clerking to take a position in the office of the clerk of the High Court of Chancery. There he became interested in law, and by reading and study began at once to supplement the scanty education of his childhood. To such good purpose did he use his opportunities that in 1797, when only twenty years old, he was licensed by the judges of the court of appeals to practice law.

When he moved from Richmond to Lexington, Kentucky, the same year to begin practice for himself, he had no influential friends, no patrons, and not even the means to pay his board. Referring to this time years afterward, he said, "I remember how comfortable I thought I should be if I could make one hundred pounds Virginia money (less than five hundred dollars) per year; and with what delight I received the first fifteen-shilling fee."

Contrary to his expectations, the young lawyer had "immediately rushed into a lucrative practice." At the age of twenty-seven he was elected to the Kentucky legislature. Two years later he was sent to the United States Senate to fill out the remainder of the term of a senator who had withdrawn. In 1811 he was elected to Congress, and made

Speaker of the national House of Representatives. He was afterward elected to the United States Senate in the regular way.

Both in Congress and in the Senate Clay always worked for what he believed to be the best interests of his country. Ambition, which so often causes men to turn aside from the paths of truth and honor, had no power to tempt him to do wrong. He was ambitious to be president, but would not sacrifice any of his convictions for the sake of being elected. Although he was nominated by his party three times, he never became president. It was when warned by a friend that if he persisted in a certain course of political conduct he would injure his prospects of being elected, that he made his famous statement, "I would rather be right than be president."

Clay has been described by one of his biographers as "a brilliant orator, an honest man, a charming gentleman, an ardent patriot, and a leader whose popularity was equaled only by that of Andrew Jackson."

Although born in a state in which wealth and ancient ancestry were highly rated, he was never ashamed of his birth or poverty. Once when taunted by the aristocratic John Randolph with his lowly origin, he proudly exclaimed, "I was born to no proud paternal estate. I inherited only infancy, ignorance, and indigence."

He was born in Hanover County, Virginia, on April 12, 1777, and died in Washington, June 29, 1852. With only the humble inheritance which he claimed—"infancy, ignorance, and indigence"—Henry Clay made himself a name that wealth and a long line of ancestry could never bestow.

***

THE GREEK SLAVE WHO WON THE OLIVE CROWN

The teeming life of the streets has vanished; the voices of the children have died away into silence; the artisan has dropped his tools, the artist has laid aside his brush, the sculptor his chisel. Night has spread her wings over the scene. The queen city of Greece is wrapped in slumber.

But, in the midst of that hushed life, there is one who sleeps not, a worshiper at the shrine of art, who feels neither fatigue nor hardship, and fears not death itself in the pursuit of his object. With the fire of genius burning in his dark eyes, a youth works with feverish haste on a group of wondrous beauty.

But why is this master artist at work, in secret, in a cellar where the sun never shone, the daylight never entered? I will tell you. Creon, the inspired worker, the son of genius, is a slave, and the penalty of pursuing his art is death.

When the Athenian law debarring all but freemen from the exercise of art was enacted, Creon was at work trying to realize in marble the vision his soul had created. The beautiful group was growing into life under his magic touch when the cruel edict struck the chisel from his fingers.

"O ye gods!" groans the stricken youth, "why have ye deserted me, now, when my task is almost completed? I have thrown my soul, my very life, into this block of marble, and now—"

Cleone, the beautiful dark-haired sister of the sculptor, felt the blow as keenly as her brother, to whom she was utterly devoted. "O immortal Athene! my goddess, my patron, at whose shrine I have daily laid my offerings, be now my friend, the friend of my brother!" she prayed.

Then, with the light of a new-born resolve shining in her eyes, she turned to her brother, saying:—

"The thought of your brain shall live. Let us go to the cellar beneath our house. It is dark, but I will bring you light and food, and no one will discover our secret. You can there continue your work; the gods will be our allies."

It is the golden age of Pericles, the most brilliant epoch of Grecian art and dramatic literature.

The scene is one of the most memorable that has ever been enacted within the proud city of Athens.

In the Agora, the public assembly or market place, are gathered together the wisdom and wit, the genius and beauty, the glory and power, of all Greece.

Enthroned in regal state sits Pericles, president of the assembly, soldier, statesman, orator, ruler, and "sole master of Athens." By his side sits his beautiful partner, the learned and queenly Aspasia. Phidias, one of the greatest sculptors, if not the greatest the world has known, who "formed a new style characterized by sublimity and ideal beauty," is there. Near him is Sophocles, the greatest of the tragic poets. Yonder we catch a glimpse of a face and form that offers the most striking contrast to the manly beauty of the poet, but whose wisdom and virtue have brought Athens to his feet. It is the "father of philosophy," Socrates. With his arm linked in that of the philosopher, we see—but why prolong the list? All Greece has been bidden to Athens to view the works of art.

The works of the great masters are there. On every side paintings and statues, marvelous in detail, exquisite in finish, challenge the admiration of the crowd and the criticism of the rival artists and connoisseurs who throng the place. But even in the midst of masterpieces, one group of statuary so far surpasses all the others that it rivets the attention of the vast assembly.

"Who is the sculptor of this group?" demands Pericles. Envious artists look from one to the other with questioning eyes, but the question remains unanswered. No triumphant sculptor comes forward to claim the wondrous creation as the work of his brain and hand. Heralds, in thunder tones, repeat, "Who is the sculptor of this group?" No one can tell. It is a mystery. Is it the work of the gods? or—and, with bated breath, the question passes from lip to lip, "Can it have been fashioned by the hand of a slave?"

Suddenly a disturbance arises at the edge of the crowd. Loud voices are heard, and anon the trembling tones of a woman. Pushing their way through the concourse, two officers drag a shrinking girl, with dark, frightened eyes, to the feet of Pericles. "This woman," they cry, "knows the sculptor; we are sure of this; but she will not tell his name."

Neither threats nor pleading can unlock the lips of the brave girl. Not even when informed that the penalty of her conduct was death would she divulge her secret. "The law," says Pericles, "is imperative. Take the maid to the dungeon."

Creon, who, with his sister, had been among the first to find his way to the Agora that morning, rushed forward, and, flinging himself at the ruler's feet, cried "O Pericles! forgive and save the maid. She is my sister. I am the culprit. The group is the work of my hands, the hands of a slave."

An intense silence fell upon the multitude, and then went up a mighty shout,—"To the dungeon, to the dungeon with the slave."

"As I live, no!" said Pericles, rising. "Not to the dungeon, but to my side bring the youth. The highest purpose of the law should be the development of the beautiful. The gods decide by that group that there is something higher in Greece than an unjust law. To the sculptor who fashioned it give the victor's crown."

And then, amid the applause of all the people, Aspasia placed the crown of olives on the youth's brow, and tenderly kissed the devoted sister who had been the right hand of genius.

***

TURNING POINTS IN THE LIFE OF A HERO

I. THE FIRST TURNING POINT

David Farragut was acting as cabin boy to his father, who was on his way to New Orleans with the infant navy of the United States. The boy thought he had the qualities that make a man. "I could swear like an old salt," he says, "could drink as stiff a glass of grog as if I had doubled Cape Horn, and could smoke like a locomotive. I was great at cards, and was fond of gambling in every shape. At the close of dinner one day," he continues, "my father turned everybody out of the cabin, locked the door, and said to me, 'David, what do you mean to be?'

"'I mean to follow the sea,' I said.

"'Follow the sea!' exclaimed father, 'yes, be a poor, miserable, drunken sailor before the mast, kicked and cuffed about the world, and die in some fever hospital in a foreign clime!'

"'No, father,' I replied, 'I will tread the quarterdeck, and command as you do.'

"'No, David; no boy ever trod the quarterdeck with such principles as you have and such habits as you exhibit. You will have to change your whole course of life if you ever become a man.'

"My father left me and went on deck. I was stunned by the rebuke, and overwhelmed with mortification. 'A poor, miserable, drunken sailor before the mast, kicked and cuffed about the world, and die in some fever hospital!' 'That's my fate, is it? I'll change my life, and I WILL CHANGE IT AT ONCE. I will never utter another oath, never drink another drop of intoxicating liquor, never gamble,' and, as God is my witness," said the admiral, solemnly, "I have kept these three vows to this hour."

II. A BORN LEADER

The event which proved David Glasgow Farragut's qualities as a leader happened before he was thirteen.

He was with his adopted father, Captain Porter, on board the Essex, when war was declared with England in 1812. A number of prizes were captured by the Essex, and David was ordered by Captain Porter to take one of the captured vessels, with her commander as navigator, to Valparaiso. Although inwardly quailing before the violent-tempered old captain of the prize ship, of whom, as he afterward confessed, he was really "a little afraid," the boy assumed the command with a fearless air.

On giving his first order, that the "main topsail be filled away," the trouble began. The old captain, furious at hearing a command given aboard his vessel by a boy not yet in his teens, replied to the order, with an oath, that he would shoot any one who dared touch a rope without his orders. Having delivered this mandate, he rushed below for his pistols.

The situation was critical. If the young commander hesitated for a moment, or showed the least sign of submitting to be bullied, his authority would instantly have fallen from him. Boy as he was, David realized this, and, calling one of the crew to him, explained what had taken place, and repeated his order. With a hearty "Aye, aye, sir!" the sailor flew to the ropes, while the plucky midshipman called down to the captain that "if he came on deck with his pistols, he would be thrown overboard."

David's victory was complete. During the remainder of the voyage none dared dispute his authority. Indeed his coolness and promptitude had won for him the lasting admiration of the crew.

III. "FARRAGUT IS THE MAN"

The great turning point which placed Farragut at the head of the American navy was reached in 1861, when Virginia seceded from the Union, and he had to choose between the cause of the North and that of the South. He dearly loved his native South, and said, "God forbid that I should have to raise my hand against her," but he determined, come what would, to "stick to the flag."

So it came about that when, in order to secure the control of the Mississippi, the national government resolved upon the capture of New Orleans, Farragut was chosen to lead the undertaking. Several officers, noted for their loyalty, good judgment, and daring, were suggested, but the Secretary of the Navy said, "Farragut is the man."

The opportunity for which all his previous noble life and brilliant services had been a preparation came to him when he was sixty-one years old. The command laid upon him was "the certain capture of the city of New Orleans." "The department and the country," so ran his instructions, "require of you success. ... If successful, you open the way to the sea for the great West, never again to be closed. The rebellion will be riven in the center, and the flag, to which you have been so faithful, will recover its supremacy in every state."

On January 9, 1862, Farragut was appointed to the command of the western gulf blockading squadron. "On February 2," says the National Cyclopedia of American Biograph, "he sailed on the steam sloop Hartford from Hampton Roads, arriving at the appointed rendezvous, Ship Island, in sixteen days. His fleet, consisting of six war steamers, sixteen gunboats, twenty-one mortar vessels, under the command of Commodore David D. Porter, and five supply ships, was the largest that had ever sailed under the American flag. Yet the task assigned him, the passing of the forts below New Orleans, the capture of the city, and the opening of the Mississippi River through its entire length was one of difficulty unprecedented in the history of naval warfare."

Danger or death had no terror for the brave sailor. Before setting out on his hazardous enterprise, he said: "If I die in the attempt, it will only be what every officer has to expect. He who dies in doing his duty to his country, and at peace with his God, has played the drama of life to the best advantage."

The hero did not die. He fought and won the great battle, and thus executed the command laid upon him,—"the certain capture of the city of New Orleans." The victory was accomplished with the loss of but one ship, and 184 men killed and wounded,—"a feat in naval warfare," says his son and biographer, "which has no precedent, and which is still without a parallel, except the one furnished by Farragut himself, two years later, at Mobile."

***

HE AIMED HIGH AND HIT THE MARK

"Without vision the people perish"

Without a high ideal an individual never climbs. Keep your eyes on the mountain top, and, though you may stumble and fall many times in the ascent, though great bowlders, dense forests, and roaring torrents may often bar the way, look right on, never losing sight of the light which shines away up in the clear atmosphere of the mountain peak, and you will ultimately reach your goal.

When the late Horace Maynard, LL.D., entered Amherst College, he exposed himself to the ridicule and jibing questions of his fellow-students by placing over the door of his room a large square of white cardboard on which was inscribed in bold outlines the single letter "V." Disregarding comment and question, the young man applied himself to his work, ever keeping in mind the height to which he wished to climb, the first step toward which was signified by the mysterious "V."

Four years later, after receiving the compliments of professors and students on the way he had acquitted himself as valedictorian of his class, young Maynard called the attention of his fellow-graduates to the letter over his door. Then a light broke in upon them, and they cried out, "Is it possible that you had the valedictory in mind when you put that 'V' over your door?"

"Assuredly I had," was the emphatic reply.

On he climbed, from height to height, becoming successively professor of mathematics in the University of Tennessee, lawyer, member of Congress, attorney-general of Tennessee, United States minister to Constantinople, and, finally, postmaster-general.

Honorable ambition is the leaven that raises the whole mass of mankind. Ideals, visions, are the stepping-stones by which we rise to higher things.

"Still, through our paltry stir and strife,
  Glows down the wished ideal,
And longing molds in clay what life
  Carves in the marble real;

"To let the new life in, we know,
  Desire must ope the portal,—
Perhaps the longing to be so
  Helps make the soul immortal."

***

THE EVOLUTION OF A VIOLINIST

He was a famous artist whom kings and queens and emperors delighted to honor. The emperor of all the Russias had sent him an affectionate letter, written by his own hand; the empress, a magnificent emerald ring set with diamonds; the king of his own beloved Norway, who had listened reverently, standing with uncovered head, while he, the king of violinists, played before him, had bestowed upon him the Order of Vasa; the king of Copenhagen presented him with a gold snuffbox, encrusted with diamonds; while, at a public dinner given him by the students of Christiana, he was crowned with a laurel wreath. Not all the thousands who thronged to hear him in London could gain entrance to the concert hall, and in Liverpool he received four thousand dollars for one evening's performance.

Yet the homage of the great ones of the earth, the princely gifts bestowed upon him, the admiration of the thousands who hung entranced on every note breathed by his magic violin, gave less delight than the boy of fourteen experienced when he received from an old man, whose heart his playing had gladdened, the present of four pairs of doves, with a card suspended by a blue ribbon round the neck of one, bearing his own name, "Ole Bull."

The soul of little Ole Bull had always been attuned to melody, from the time when, a toddling boy of four, he had kissed with passionate delight the little yellow violin given him by his uncle. How happy he was, as he wandered alone through the meadows, listening with the inner ear of heaven-born genius to the great song of nature. The bluebells, the buttercups, and the blades of grass sang to him in low, sweet tones, unheard by duller ears. How he thrilled with delight when he touched the strings of the little red violin, purchased for him when he was eight years old. His father destined him for the church, and, feeling that music should form part of the education of a clergyman, he consented to the mother's proposition that the boy should take lessons on the violin.

Ole could not sleep for joy, that first night of ownership; and, when the house was wrapped in slumber, he got up and stole on tiptoe to the room where his treasure lay. The bow seemed to beckon to him, the pretty pearl screws to smile at him out of their red setting. "I pinched the strings just a little," he said. "It smiled at me ever more and more. I took up the bow and looked at it. It said to me it would be pleasant to try it across the strings. So I did try it just a very, very little, and it did sing to me so sweetly. At first I did play very soft. But presently I did begin a capriccio, which I like very much, and it did go ever louder and louder; and I forgot that it was midnight and that everybody was asleep. Presently I hear something crack; and the next minute I feel my father's whip across my shoulders. My little red violin dropped on the floor, and was broken. I weep much for it, but it did no good. They did have a doctor to it next day, but it never recovered its health."

He was given another violin, however, and, when only ten, he would wander into the fields and woods, and spend hours playing his own improvisations, echoing the song of the birds, the murmur of the brook, the thunder of the waterfall, the soughing of the wind among the trees, the roar of the storm.

But childhood's days are short. The years fly by. The little Ole is eighteen, a student in the University of Christiana, preparing for the ministry. His brother students beg him to play for a charitable association. He remembers his father's request that he yield not to his passion for music, but being urged for "sweet charity's sake," he consents.

The youth's struggle between the soul's imperative demand and the equally imperative parental dictate was pathetic. Meanwhile the position of musical director of the Philharmonic and Dramatic Societies becoming vacant, Ole was appointed to the office; and, seeing that it was useless to contend longer against the genius of his son, the disappointed father allowed him to accept the directorship.

When fairly launched on a musical career, his trials and disappointments began. Wishing to assure himself whether he had genius or not, he traveled five hundred miles to see and hear the celebrated Louis Spohr, who received the tremulous youth coldly, and gave him no encouragement. No matter, he would go to the city of art. In Paris he heard Berlioz and other great musicians. Entranced he listened, in his high seat at the top of the house, to the exquisite notes of Malibran.

His soul feasted on music, but his money was fast dwindling away, and the body could not be sustained by sweet sounds. But the poor unknown violinist, who was only another atom in the surging life of the great city, could earn nothing. He was on the verge of starvation, but he would not go back to Christiana. He must still struggle and study. He became ill of brain fever, and was tenderly nursed back to life by the granddaughter of his kind landlady, pretty little Felicie Villeminot, who afterward became his wife. He had drained the cup of poverty and disappointment to the dregs, but the tide was about to turn.

He was invited to play at a concert presided over by the Duke of Montebello, and this led to other profitable engagements. But the great opportunity of his life came to him in Bologna. The people had thronged to the opera house to hear Malibran. She had disappointed them, and they were in no mood to be lenient to the unknown violinist who had the temerity to try to fill her place.

He came on the stage. He bowed. He grew pale under the cold gaze of the thousands of unsympathetic eyes turned upon him. But the touch of his beloved violin gave him confidence. Lovingly, tenderly, he drew the bow across the strings. The coldly critical eyes no longer gazed at him. The unsympathetic audience melted away. He and his violin were one and alone. In the hands of the great magician the instrument was more than human. It talked; it laughed; it wept; it controlled the moods of men as the wind controls the sea.

The audience scarcely breathed. Criticism was disarmed. Malibran was forgotten. The people were under the spell of the enchanter. Orpheus had come again. But suddenly the music ceased. The spell was broken. With a shock the audience returned to earth, and Ole Bull, restored to consciousness of his whereabouts by the storm of applause which shook the house, found himself famous forever.

His triumph was complete, but his work was not over, for the price of fame is ceaseless endeavor. But the turning point had been passed. He had seized the great opportunity for which his life had been a preparation, and it had placed him on the roll of the immortals.

***

THE LESSON OF THE TEAKETTLE

The teakettle was singing merrily over the fire; the good aunt was bustling round, on housewifely cares intent, and her little nephew sat dreamily gazing into the glowing blaze on the kitchen hearth.

Presently the teakettle ceased singing, and a column of steam came rushing from its pipe. The boy started to his feet, raised the lid from the kettle, and peered in at the bubbling, boiling water, with a look of intense interest. Then he rushed off for a teacup, and, holding it over the steam, eagerly watched the latter as it condensed and formed into tiny drops of water on the inside of the cup.

Returning from an upper room, whither her duties had called her, the thrifty aunt was shocked to find her nephew engaged in so profitless an occupation, and soundly scolded him for what she called his trifling. The good lady little dreamed that James Watt was even then unconsciously studying the germ of the science by which he "transformed the steam engine from a mere toy into the most wonderful instrument which human industry has ever had at its command."

This studious little Scottish lad, who, because too frail to go to school, had been taught at home, was very different from other boys. When only six or seven years old, he would lie for hours on the hearth, in the little cottage at Greenock, near Glasgow, where he was born in 1736, drawing geometrical figures with pieces of colored chalk. He loved, too, to gaze at the stars, and longed to solve their mysteries. But his favorite pastime was to burrow among the ropes and sails and tackles in his father's store, trying to find out how they were made and what purposes they served.

In spite of his limited advantages and frail health, at fifteen he was the wonder of the public school, which he had attended for two years. His favorite studies were mathematics and natural philosophy. He had also made good progress in chemistry, physiology, mineralogy, and botany, and, at the same time, had learned carpentry and acquired some skill as a worker in metals.

So studious and ambitious a youth scarcely needed the spur of poverty to induce him to make the most of his talents. The spur was there, however, and, at the age of eighteen, though delicate in health, he was obliged to go out and battle with the world.

Having first spent some time in Glasgow, learning how to make mathematical instruments, he determined to go to London, there to perfect himself in his trade.

Working early and late, and suffering frequently from cold and hunger, he broke down under the unequal strain, and was obliged to return to his parents for a time until health was regained.

Always struggling against great odds, he returned to Glasgow when his trade was mastered, and began to make mathematical instruments, for which, however, he found little sale. Then, to help eke out a living, he began to make and mend other instruments,—fiddles, guitars, and flutes,—and finally built an organ,—a very superior one, too,—with several additions of his own invention.

A commonplace incident enough it seemed, in the routine of his daily occupation, when, one morning, a model of Newcomen's engine was brought to him for repair, yet it marked the turning point in his career, which ultimately led from poverty and struggle to fame and affluence.

Watt's practiced eye at once perceived the defects in the Newcomen engine, which, although the best then in existence could not do much better or quicker work than horses. Filled with enthusiasm over the plans which he had conceived for the construction of a really powerful engine, he immediately set to work, and spent two months in an old cellar, working on a model. "My whole thoughts are bent on this machine," he wrote to a friend. "I can think of nothing else."

So absorbed had he become in his new work that the old business of making and mending instruments had declined. This was all the more unfortunate as he was no longer struggling for himself alone. He had fallen in love with, and married, his cousin, Margaret Miller, who brought him the greatest happiness of his life. The neglect of the only practical means of support he had reduced Watt and his family to the direst poverty. More than once his health failed, and often the brave spirit was almost broken, as when he exclaimed in heaviness of heart, "Of all the things in the world, there is nothing so foolish as inventing."

Five years had passed since the model of the Newcomen engine had been sent to him for repair before he succeeded in securing a patent on his own invention. Yet five more long years of bitter drudgery, clutched in the grip of poverty, debt, and sickness, did the brave inventor, sustained by the love and help of his noble wife, toil through. On his thirty-fifth birthday he said, "To-day I enter the thirty-fifth year of my life, and I think I have hardly yet done thirty-five pence worth of good in the world; but I cannot help it."

Poor Watt! He had traveled with bleeding feet along the same thorny path trod by the great inventors and benefactors of all ages. But, in spite of all obstacles, he persevered; and, after ten years of inconceivable labor and hardship, during which his beautiful wife died, he had a glorious triumph. His perfected steam engine was the wonder of the age. Sir James Mackintosh placed him "at the head of all inventors in all ages and nations." "I look upon him," said the poet Wordsworth, "considering both the magnitude and the universality of his genius, as, perhaps, the most extraordinary man that this country ever produced."

Wealthy beyond his desires,—for he cared not for wealth,—crowned with the laurel wreath of fame, honored by the civilized world as one of its greatest benefactors, the struggle over, the triumph achieved, on August 19, 1819, he lay down to rest.

***

HOW THE ART OF PRINTING WAS DISCOVERED

"Look, Grandfather; see what the letters have done!" exclaimed a delighted boy, as he picked up the piece of parchment in which Grandfather Coster had carried the bark letters cut from the trees in the grove, for the instruction and amusement of his little grandsons.

"See what the letters have done!" echoed the old man. "Bless me, what does the child mean?" and his eyes twinkled with pleasure, as he noted the astonishment and pleasure visible on the little face. "Let me see what it is that pleases thee so, Laurence," and he eagerly took the parchment from the boy's hand.

"Bless my soul!" cried the old man, after gazing spellbound upon it for some seconds. The track of the mysterious footprint in the sand excited no more surprise in the mind of Robinson Crusoe than Grandfather Coster felt at the sight which met his eyes. There, distinctly impressed upon the parchment, was a clear imprint of the bark letters; though, of course, they were reversed or turned about.

But you twentieth-century young folks who have your fill of story books, picture books, and reading matter of all kinds, are wondering, perhaps, what all this talk about bark letters and parchment and imprint of letters means.

To understand it, you must carry your imagination away back more than five centuries—quite a long journey of the mind, even for "grown-ups"—to a time when there were no printed books, and when very, very few of the rich and noble, and scarcely any of the so-called common people, could read. In those far-off days there were no public libraries, and no books except rare and expensive volumes, written by hand, mainly by monks in their quiet monasteries, on parchment or vellum.

In the quaint, drowsy, picturesque town of Haarlem, in Holland, with its narrow, irregular, grass-grown streets and many-gabled houses, the projecting upper stories of which almost meet, one particular house, which seems even older than any of the others, is pointed out to visitors as one of the most interesting sights of the ancient place. It was in this house that Laurence Coster, the father of the art of printing, the man—at least so runs the legend—who made it possible for the poorest and humblest to enjoy the inestimable luxury of books and reading, lived and loved and dreamed more than five hundred years ago.

Coster was warden of the little church which stood near his home, and his days flowed peacefully on, in a quiet, uneventful way, occupied with the duties of his office, and reading and study, for he was one of those who had mastered the art of reading. A diligent student, he had conned over and over, until he knew them by heart, the few manuscript volumes owned by the little church of which he was warden.

A lover of solitude, as well as student and dreamer, the church warden's favorite resort, when his duties left him at leisure, was a dense grove not far from the town. Thither he went when he wished to be free from all distraction, to think and dream over many things which would appear nonsensical to his sober, practical-minded neighbors. There he indulged in day dreams and poetic fancies; and once, when in a sentimental mood, he carved the initials of the lady of his love on one of the trees.

In time a fair young wife and children came, bringing new brightness and joy to the serious-minded warden. With ever increasing interests, he passed on from youth to middle life, and from middle life to old age. Then his son married, and again the patter of little feet filled the old home and made music in the ears of Grandfather Coster, whom the baby grandchildren almost worshiped.

To amuse the children, and to impart to them whatever knowledge he himself possessed, became the delight of his old age. Then the habit acquired in youth of carving letters in the bark of the trees served a very useful purpose in furthering his object. He still loved to take solitary walks, and many a quiet summer afternoon the familiar figure of the venerable churchwarden, in his seedy black cloak and sugar-loaf hat, might be seen wending its way along the banks of the River Spaaren to his favorite resort in the grove.

One day, while reclining on a mossy couch beneath a spreading beech tree, amusing himself by tearing strips of bark from the tree that shaded him, and carving letters with his knife, a happy thought entered his mind. "Why can I not," he mused within himself, "cut those letters out, carry them home, and, while using them as playthings, teach the little ones how to read?"

The plan worked admirably. Long practice had made the old man quite expert in fashioning the letters, and many hours of quiet happiness were spent in the grove in this pleasing occupation. One afternoon he succeeded in cutting some unusually fine specimens, and, chuckling to himself over the delight they would give the children, he wrapped them carefully, placing them side by side in an old piece of parchment which he happened to have in his pocket. The bark from which they had been cut being fresh and full of sap, and the letters being firmly pressed upon the parchment, the result was the series of "pictures" which delighted the child and gave to the world the first suggestion of a printing press.

And then a mighty thought flashed across the brain of the poor, humble, unknown churchwarden, a thought the realization of which was destined not only to make him famous for all time, but to revolutionize the whole world. The first dim suggestion came to him in this form, "By having a series of letters and impressing them over and over again on parchment, cannot books be printed instead of written, and so multiplied and cheapened as to be brought within the reach of all?"

The remainder of his life was given up to developing this great idea. He cut more letters from bark, and, covering the smooth surface with ink, pressed them upon parchment, thus getting a better impression, though still blurred and imperfect. He then cut letters from wood instead of bark, and managed to invent himself a better and thicker ink, which did not blur the page. Next, he cut letters from lead, and then from pewter. Every hour was absorbed in the work of making possible the art of printing. His simple-minded neighbors thought he had lost his mind, and some of the more superstitious spread the report that he was a sorcerer. But, like all other great discoverers, he heeded not annoyances or discouragements. Shutting himself away from the prying curiosity of the ignorant and superstitious, he plodded on, making steady, if slow, advance toward the realization of his dream.

"One day, while old Coster was thus busily at work," says George Makepeace Towle, "a sturdy German youth, with a knapsack slung across his back, trudged into Haarlem. By some chance this youth happened to hear how the churchwarden was at work upon a wild scheme to print books instead of writing them. With beating heart, the young man repaired to Coster's house and made all haste to knock at the churchwarden's humble door."

The "sturdy German youth" who knocked at Laurence Coster's door was Johann Gutenberg, the inventor of modern printing. Coster invited him to enter. Gutenberg accepted the invitation, and then stated the object of his visit. He desired to learn more about the work on which Coster was engaged. Delighted to have a visitor who was honestly interested in his work, the old man eagerly explained its details to the youth, and showed him some examples of his printing.

Gutenberg was much impressed by what he saw, but still more by the possibilities which he dimly foresaw in Coster's discovery. "But we can do much better than this," he said with the enthusiasm of youth. "Your printing is even slower than the writing of the monks. From this day forth I will work upon this problem, and not rest till I have solved it."

Johann Gutenberg kept his word. He never rested until he had given the art of printing to the world. But to Laurence Coster, in the first place, if legend speaks truth, we owe one of the greatest inventions that has ever blessed mankind.

***

SEA FEVER AND WHAT IT LED TO

"Jim, you've too good a head on you to be a wood chopper or a canal driver," said the captain of the canal boat for whom young Garfield had engaged to drive horses along the towpath.

"Jim" had always loved books from the time when, seated on his father's knee, he had with his baby lips pronounced after him the name "Plutarch." Mr. Garfield had been reading "Plutarch's Lives," and was much astonished when, without hesitation or stammering, his little son distinctly pronounced the name of the Greek biographer. Turning to his wife, with a glow of love and pride, the fond father said, "Eliza, this boy will be a scholar some day."

Perhaps the near approach of death had clarified the father's vision, but when, soon after, the sorrowing wife was left a widow, with an indebted farm and four little children to care for, she saw little chance for the fulfillment of the prophecy.

Even in his babyhood the boy whose future greatness the father dimly felt had learned the lesson of self-reliance. The familiar words which so often fell from his lips—"I can do that"—enabled him to conquer difficulties before which stouter hearts than that of a little child might well have quailed.

The teaching of his good mother, that "God will bless all our efforts to do the best we can," became a part of the fiber of his being. "What will He do," asked the boy one day, "when we don't do the best we can?" "He will withhold His blessing; and that is the greatest calamity that could possibly happen to us," was the reply, which made a deep impression on the mind of the questioner.

In spite of almost constant toil, and very meager schooling,—only a few weeks each year,—James Garfield excelled all his companions in the log schoolhouse. Besides solving at home in the long winter evenings, by the light of the pine fire, all the knotty problems in Adams' Arithmetic—the terror of many a schoolboy—he found time to revel in the pages of "Robinson Crusoe" and "Josephus." The latter was his special favorite.

Before he was fifteen, Garfield had successfully followed the occupations of farmer, wood chopper, and carpenter. No matter what his occupation was he always managed to find some time for reading.

He had recently read some of Marryat's novels, "Sindbad the Sailor," "The Pirate's Own Book," and others of a similar nature, which had smitten him with a virulent attack of sea fever. This is a mental disease which many robust, adventurous boys are apt to contract in their teens. Garfield felt that he must "sail the ocean blue." The glamour of the sea was upon him. Everything must give way before it. His mother, however, could not be induced to assent to his plans, and, after long pleading, would only compromise by agreeing that he might, if he could, secure a berth on one of the vessels navigating Lake Erie.

He was rudely repulsed by the owner of the first vessel to whom he applied, a brutal, drunken creature, who answered his request for employment with an oath and a rough "Get off this schooner in double quick, or I'll throw you into the dock." Garfield turned away in disgust, his ardor for the sea somewhat dampened by the man's appearance and behavior. In this mood he met his cousin, formerly a schoolmaster, then captain of a canal boat, with whom he at once engaged to drive his horses.

After a few months on the towpath, young Garfield contracted another kind of fever quite unlike that from which he had been suffering previously, and went home to be nursed out of it by his ever faithful mother.

During his convalescence he thought a great deal over his cousin's words,—"Jim, you've got too good a head on you to be a wood chopper or a canal driver." "He who wills to do anything will do it," he had learned from his mother's lips when a mere baby, and then and there he said in his heart, "I will be a scholar; I will go to college." And so, out of his sea fever and towpath experience was born the resolution that made the turning point in his career.

Action followed hot upon resolve. He lost no time in applying himself to the work of securing an education. Alternately chopping wood and carpentering, farming and teaching school, ringing bells and sweeping floors, he worked his way through seminary and college. His strong will and resolute purpose to make the most of himself not only enabled him to obtain an education, but raised him from the towpath to the presidential chair.

***

GLADSTONE FOUND TIME TO BE KIND

A kindly act is a kernel sown,
That will grow to a goodly tree,
Shedding its fruit when time has flown
Down the gulf of Eternity.

JOHN BOYLE O'REILLY.

In the restless desire for acquisition,—acquisition of money, of power, or of fame,—there is danger of selfishness, self-absorption, closing the doors of our hearts against the demands of brotherly love, courtesy, and kindness.

"I cannot afford to help," say the poor in pocket; "all I have is too little for my own needs." "I should like to help others," says the ambitious student, whose every spare moment is crowded with some extra task, "but I have no money, and cannot afford to take the time from my studies to give sympathy or kind words to the suffering and the poor." Says the busy man of affairs: "I am willing to give money, but my time is too valuable to be spent in talking to sick people or shiftless, lazy ones. That sort of work is not in my line. I leave it to women and the charitable organizations."

The business man forgets, as do many of us, the truth expressed by Ruskin, that "a little thought and a little kindness are often worth more than a great deal of money." A few kind words, a little sympathy and encouragement have often brought sunshine and hope into the lives of men and women who were on the verge of despair.

The great demand is on people's hearts rather than on their purses. In the matter of kindness we can all afford to be generous whether we have money or not. The schoolboy may give it as freely as the millionaire. No one is so driven by work that he has not time, now and then, to say a kind word or do a kind deed that will help to brighten life for another. If the prime minister of England, William E. Gladstone, could find time to carry a bunch of flowers to a little sick crossing-sweeper, shall we not be ashamed to make for ourselves the excuse, "I haven't time to be kind"?

***

A TRIBUNE OF THE PEOPLE

Clad in a homespun tow shirt, shrunken, butternut-colored, linsey-woolsey pantaloons, battered straw hat, and much-mended jacket and shoes, with ten dollars in his pocket, and all his other worldly goods packed in the bundle he carried on his back, Horace Greeley, the future founder of the New York Tribune, started to seek his fortune in New York.

A newspaper had always been an object of interest and delight to the little delicate, tow-haired boy, and at the mature age of six he had made up his mind to be a printer. His love of reading was unusual in one so young. Before he was six he had read the Bible and "Pilgrim's Progress" through.

Like the children of all poor farmers, Horace was put to work as soon as he was able to do anything. But he made the most of the opportunities given him to attend school, and his love of reading; stimulated him to unusual efforts to procure books. By selling nuts and bundles of kindling wood at the village store, before he was ten he had earned enough money to buy a copy of Shakespeare and of Mrs. Hemans's poems. He borrowed every book that could be found within a radius of seven miles of his home, and by many readings he had made himself familiar with the score of old volumes in his log-cabin home.

Mrs. Sarah K. Bolton draws a pleasing picture of the farmer boy reading at night after the day's work on the farm was done. "He gathered a stock of pine knots," she says, "and, lighting one each night, lay down by the hearth and read, oblivious to all around him. The neighbors came and made their friendly visits, and ate apples and drank cider, as was the fashion, but the lad never noticed their coming or their going. When really forced to leave his precious books for bed, he would repeat the information he had learned, or the lessons for the next day to his brother, who usually, most ungraciously, fell asleep before the conversation was half completed."

"Ah!" said Zaccheus Greeley, Horace's father, when the boy one day, in a fit of abstraction, tried to yoke the "off" ox on the "near" side: "Ah! that boy will never know enough to get on in the world. He'll never know more than enough to come in when it rains!"

Yet this boy knew so much that when at fourteen he secured a place as printer in a newspaper office at East Poultney, Vermont, he was looked up to by his fellow-printers as equal in learning to the editor himself.

At first they tried to make merry at his expense, poking fun at his odd-looking garments, his uncouth appearance, and his pale, delicate face and almost white hair, which subsequently won for him the nickname of "Ghost." But when they saw that Horace was too good humored and too much in earnest with his work to be disturbed by their teasing, they gave it up. In a short time he became a general favorite, not only in the office, but in the town of Poultney, whose debating and literary societies soon recognized him as leader. Even the minister, the lawyer, and the school-teachers looked up to the poor, retiring young printer, who was a veritable encyclopedia of knowledge, ready at all times to speak or to write an essay on any subject.

But the Poultney newspaper was obliged to suspend soon after Horace had learned his trade, and, penniless,—for every cent of his earnings beyond what furnished the bare necessaries of life had been sent home to his parents in the wilderness,—he faced the world once more.

After working in different small towns wherever he could get a "job," reading, studying, enlarging his knowledge all the time when not in the office, he made up his mind to go to New York, "to be somebody," as he put it.

When he stepped off the towboat at Whitehall, near the Battery, that sunny morning in August, 1831, with only the experience of a score of years in life, a stout heart, quick brain, nimble fingers, and an abiding faith in God as his capital, his prospects certainly were not very alluring.

"An overgrown, awkward, white-headed, forlorn-looking boy; a pack suspended on a staff over his right shoulder; his dress unrivaled in sylvan simplicity since the primitive fig leaves of Eden; the expression of his face presenting a strange union of wonder and apathy: his whole appearance gave you the impression of a runaway apprentice in desperate search of employment. Ignorant alike of the world and its ways, he seemed to the denizens of the city almost like a wanderer from another planet."

Such was the impression Horace Greeley made on a New Yorker on his first arrival in that city which was to be the scene of his future work and triumphs.

He tramped the streets all that day, Friday, and the next, looking for work, everywhere getting the same discouraging reply, "No, we don't want any one."

At last, when weary and disheartened, his ten dollars almost gone, he had decided to shake the dust of New York from his feet, the foreman of a printing office engaged him to do some work that most of the men in the office had refused to touch. The setting up of a Polyglot Testament, with involved marginal references, was something new for the supposed "green" hand from the country. But when the day was done, the young printer was no longer looked upon as "green" by his fellow-workers, for he had done more and better work than the oldest and most experienced hands who had tried the Testament.

But, oh, what hard work it was, beginning at six o'clock in the morning, and working long after the going down of the sun, by the light of a candle stuck in a bottle, to earn six dollars a week, most of which was sent to his dear ones at home.

After nearly ten years more of struggle and privation, Greeley entered upon the great work of his life—the founding and editing of the New York Tribune. He had very little money to start with, and even that little was borrowed. But he had courage, truth, honesty, a noble purpose, and rare ability and industry to supplement his small financial capital. He needed them all in the work he had undertaken, for he was handicapped not only by lack of means, but also by the opposition of some of the New York papers.

In spite of the adverse conditions he succeeded in establishing one of the greatest and most popular newspapers in the country. The Tribune became the champion of the oppressed, the guardian of justice, the defender of truth, a power for good in the land. Through his paper Greeley became a tribune of the people. No thought of making money hampered him in his work. Unselfishly he wrought as editor, writer, and lecturer for the good of his country and the uplifting of mankind. "He who by voice or pen," he said, "strikes his best blow at the impostures or vices whereby our race is debased and paralyzed, may close his eyes in death, consoled and cheered by the reflection that he has done what he could for the emancipation and elevation of his kind."

Well, then, might he rejoice in his life work, for his voice and pen had to the last been active in thus serving the race.

He died on November 29, 1872, at the age of sixty-one. So great a man had Horace Greeley, the poor New Hampshire farmer boy, become that the whole nation mourned for his death. The people felt that in him they had lost one of their best friends. A workman who attended his funeral expressed the feeling of his fellow-workmen all over the land when he said, "It is little enough to lose a day for Horace Greeley who spent many a day working for us." "I've come a hundred miles to be at the funeral of Horace Greeley," said a farmer.

The great tribune had deserved well of the people and of his country.

***

THE MIGHT OF PATIENCE

Perhaps some would feel inclined to ridicule rather than applaud the patience of a poor Chinese woman who tried to make a needle from a rod of iron by rubbing it against a stone.

It is doubtful whether she succeeded or not, but, so the story runs, the sight of the worker plying her seemingly hopeless task, put new courage and determination into the heart of a young Chinese student, who, in deep despondency, stood watching her.

Because of repeated failures in his studies, ambition and hope had left him. Bitterly disappointed with himself, and despairing of ever accomplishing anything, the young man had thrown his books aside in disgust. Put to shame, however, by the lesson taught by the old woman, he gathered his scattered forces together, went to work with renewed ardor, and, wedding Patience and Energy, became, in time, one of the greatest scholars in China.

When you know you are on the right track, do not let any failures dim your vision or discourage you, for you cannot tell how close you may be to victory. Have patience and stick, stick, stick. It is eternally true that he

"Who steers right on

Will gain, at length, however far, the port."

***

THE INSPIRATION OF GAMBETTA

"Try to come home a somebody!" Long after Leon Gambetta had left the old French town of Cahors, where he was born October 30, 1838, long after the gay and brilliant streets of Paris had become familiar to him, did the parting words of his idolized mother ring in his ears, "Try to come home a somebody!" Pinched for food and clothes, as he often was, while he studied early and late in his bare garret near the Sorbonne, the memory of that dear mother cheered and strengthened him.

He could still feel her tears and kisses on his cheek, and the tender clasp of her hand as she pressed into his the slender purse of money which she had saved to release him from the drudgery of an occupation he loathed, and to enable him to become a great lawyer in Paris. How well he remembered her delight in listening to him declaim the speeches of Thiers and Guizot from the pages of the National, which she had taught him to read when but a mere baby, and from which he imbibed his first lessons in republicanism,—lessons that he never afterward forgot.

Such deep root had they taken that he could not be induced to change his views by the fathers of the preparatory school at Monfaucon, whither he had been sent to be trained for the priesthood. Finally despairing of bringing the young radical to their way of thinking, the Monfaucon fathers sent him home to his parents. "You will never make a priest of him," they wrote; "he has a character that cannot be disciplined."

His father, an honest but narrow-minded Italian, whose ideas did not soar beyond his little bazaar and grocery store, was displeased with the boy, who was then only ten years old. He could not understand how one so young dared to think his own thoughts and hold his own opinions. The neighbors held up their hands in dismay, and prophesied, "He will end his days in the Bastile." His mother wept and blamed herself and the National as the cause of all the trouble.

How little the fond mother, the disappointed father, or the gloomily foreboding neighbors dreamt to what heights those early lessons they now so bitterly deplored were to lead!

When at sixteen Leon Gambetta returned from the Lyceum to which he had been sent on his return from the Monfaucon seminary, his wide reading and deep study had but intensified and broadened the radicalism of his childhood. He longed to go to Paris to study law, but his father insisted that he must now confine his thoughts to selling groceries and yards of ribbon and lace, as he expected his son to succeed him in the business.

Poor, foolish Joseph Gambetta! he would confine the young eagle in a barnyard. But the eagle pined and drooped in his cage, and then the loving mother—ah, those loving mothers, will their boys ever realize how much they owe them!—threw open the doors and gave him freedom, an opportunity to win fame and fortune in the great city of Paris.

And now what mattered it that his clothes were poor, that his food was scant, and that it was often bitterly cold in his little garret. If not for his own sake, he MUST for hers "come home a somebody."

The doors which led to a wider future were already opening. The professors at the Sorbonne appreciated his great intellect and originality. "You have a true vocation," said one. "Follow it. But go to the bar, where your voice, which is one in a thousand, will carry you on, study and intelligence aiding. The lecture room is a narrow theater. If you like, I will write to your father to tell him what my opinion of you is." And he wrote, "The best investment you ever made would be to spend what money you can divert from your business in helping your son to become an advocate."

To such good purpose did the young student use his time that within two years he won his diploma. Still too young to be admitted to the bar, he spent a year studying life in Paris, listening to the debates in the Corps Legislatif, reading and debating in the radical club which he had organized, making himself ready at every point for the great opportunity which gained him a national reputation and made him the idol of the masses.

In 1868 his masterly defense of Delescluze, the radical editor, against the prosecution of the Imperial government, brought the brilliant but hitherto unknown young lawyer prominently before the public. He lost his case, but won fame. Gambetta had waited eighteen months for his first brief, and five times eighteen months for his first great case. This case proved to be the initial step that led him from victory to victory, until, after the fall of Napoleon at Sedan, he became practically Dictator of France. He was, more than any one man, the maker of the French Republic, whose rights and liberties he ever defended, even at the risk of his life. He died December 31, 1882.

Well had he fulfilled the hopes and ambitions of his loving mother, well had he answered the pathetic appeal, "Try to come home a somebody."

***

ANDREW JACKSON THE BOY WHO "NEVER WOULD GIVE UP"

"Sir, I am a prisoner of war, and demand to be treated as such," was the spirited reply of Andrew Jackson to a British officer who had commanded him to clean his boots.

This was characteristic of the future hero of New Orleans, and president of the United States, whose independent spirit rebelled at the insolent command of his captor.

The officer drew his sword to enforce obedience, but, nothing daunted, the youth, although then only fourteen, persisted in his refusal. He tried to parry the sword thrusts aimed at him, but did not escape without wounds on head and arm, the marks of which he carried to his grave.

Stubborn, self-willed, and always dominated by the desire to be a leader, Andrew Jackson was by no means a model boy. But his honesty, love of truth, indomitable will and courage, in spite of his many faults, led him to greatness.

He was born with fighting blood in his veins, and, like other eminent men who have risen to the White House, poor. His father, an Irish immigrant, died before his youngest son was born,—in 1767,—and life held for the boy more hard knocks than soft places. His mother, who was ambitious to make him a clergyman, tried to secure him some early advantages of schooling. Andrew, however, was not of a studious disposition, nor at all inclined to the ministry, and made little effort to profit by even the limited opportunities he had.

But despite all the disadvantages of environment and mental traits by which he was handicapped, he was bound by the force of certain other traits to be a winner in the battle of life. The quality to which his success is chiefly owing is revealed by the words of a school-fellow, who, in spite of Jackson's slender physique and lack of physical strength at that time, felt the force of his iron will. Speaking of their wrestling matches at school, this boy said, "I could throw him [Jackson] three times out of four, but he never would stay throwed. He was dead game and never would give up."

A boy who "never would stay throwed," and "never would give up" would succeed though the whole world tried to bar his progress.

When, at the age of fifteen, he found himself alone in the world, homeless and penniless, he adapted himself to anything he could find to do.

Worker in a saddler's shop, school-teacher, lawyer, merchant, judge of the Supreme Court, United States senator, soldier, leader, step by step the son of the poor Irish immigrant rose to the highest office to which his countrymen could elect him—the presidency of the United States.

Rash, headstrong, and narrow-minded, Andrew Jackson fell into many errors during his life, but, notwithstanding his shortcomings, he persistently tried to live up to his boyhood's motto, "Ask nothing but what is right—submit to nothing wrong."

***

SIR HUMPHRY DAVY'S GREATEST DISCOVERY, MICHAEL FARADAY

He was only a little, barefooted errand boy, the son of a poor blacksmith. His school life ended in his thirteenth year. The extent of his education then was limited to a knowledge of the three "R's." As he trudged on his daily rounds, through the busy streets of London, delivering newspapers and books to the customers of his employer, there was little difference, outwardly, between him and scores of other boys who jostled one another in the narrow, crowded thoroughfares. But under the shabby jacket of Michael Faraday beat a heart braver and tenderer than the average; and, under the well-worn cap, a brain was throbbing that was destined to illuminate the world of science with a light that would never grow dim.

Less than any one else, perhaps, did the boy dream of future greatness. For a year he served his employer faithfully in his capacity of errand boy, and, in 1805, at the age of fourteen, was apprenticed to a bookseller for seven years, as was the custom in England, to learn the combined trades of bookbinding and book-selling.

The young journeyman had to exercise all his self-control to confine his attention to the outside of the books which passed through his hands. In his spare moments, however, he made himself familiar with the inside of many of them, eagerly devouring such works on science, electricity, chemistry, and natural philosophy, as came within his reach. He was especially delighted with an article on electricity, which he found in a volume of the "Encyclopedia Britannica," which had been given him to bind. He immediately began work on an electrical machine, from the very crudest materials, and, much to his delight, succeeded. It was a red-letter day in his young life when a kind-hearted customer, who had noticed his interest in scientific works, offered to take him to the Royal Institution, to attend a course of lectures to be given by the great Sir Humphry Davy. From this time on, his thoughts were constantly turned toward science. "Oh, if I could only help in some scientific work, no matter how humble!" was the daily cry of his soul. But not yet was his prayer to be granted. His mettle must be tried in the school of patience and drudgery. He must fulfill his contract with his master. For seven years he was faithful to his work, while his heart was elsewhere. And all that time, in the eagerness of his thirst for knowledge, he was imbibing facts which helped him to plan electrical achievements, the possibilities of which have not, to this day, been exhausted,—or even half realized. Like Franklin, he seemed to forecast the scientific future for ages.

At length he was free to follow his bent, and his mind turned at once to Sir Humphry Davy. With a beating heart, divided between hope and fear, he wrote to the great man, telling what he wished, and asking his aid. The scientist, remembering his own day of small things, wrote the youth, politely, that he was going out of town, but would see if he could, sometime, aid him. He also said that "science is a harsh mistress, and, in a pecuniary point of view, but poorly rewards those who devote themselves exclusively to her service."

This was not very encouraging, but the young votary of science was nothing daunted, and toiled at his uncongenial trade, with the added discomfort of an ill-tempered employer, giving all his evenings and odd moments to study and experiments.

Then came another red-letter day. He was growing depressed, and feared that Sir Humphry had forgotten his quasi-promise, when one evening a carriage stopped at the door, and out stepped an important-looking footman in livery, with a note from the famous scientist, requesting the young bookbinder to call on him on the following morning. At last had come the answer to the prayer of little Michael Faraday, as will come the answer to all who back their prayers with patient, persistent hard work, in spite of discouragement, disappointment, and failure. And when, on that never-to-be-forgotten morning, he was engaged by the great scientist at a salary of six dollars a week, with two rooms at the top of the house, to wash bottles, clean the instruments, move them to and from the lecture rooms, and make himself generally useful in the laboratory and out of it, no happier youth could be found in all London.

The door was open; not, indeed, wide, but sufficiently to allow this ardent disciple to work his way into the innermost shrine of the temple of science. Though it took years and years of plodding, incessant work and study, and a devotion to purpose with which nothing was allowed to interfere, it made Faraday, by virtue of his marvelous discoveries in electricity, electro-magnetism, and chemistry, a world benefactor, honored not only by his own country and sovereign, but by other rulers and leading nations of the earth, as one of the greatest chemists and natural philosophers of his time.

So great has been his value to the scientific world, that his theories are still a constant source of inspiration to the workers in those great professions allied to electricity and chemistry. No library is complete without his published works. What wonder that Davy called Faraday his greatest discovery!

***

THE TRIUMPH OF CANOVA

The Villa d'Asola, the country residence of the Signor Falieri, was in a state of unusual excitement. Some of the most distinguished patricians of Venice had been bidden to a great banquet, which was to surpass in magnificence any entertainment ever before given, even by the wealthy and hospitable Signer Falieri.

The feast was ready, the guests were assembled, when word came from the confectioner, who had been charged to prepare the center ornament for the table, that he had spoiled the piece. Consternation reigned in the servants' hall. What was to be done? The steward, or head servant, was in despair. He was responsible for the table decorations, and the absence of the centerpiece would seriously mar the arrangements. He wrung his hands and gesticulated wildly. What should he do!

"If you will let me try, I think I can make something that will do." The speaker was a delicate, pale-faced boy, about twelve years old, who had been engaged to help in some of the minor details of preparation for the great event. "You!" exclaimed the steward, gazing in amazement at the modest, yet apparently audacious lad before him. "And who are you?" "I am Antonio Canova, the grandson of Pisano, the stonecutter." Desperately grasping at even the most forlorn hope, the perplexed servant gave the boy permission to try his hand at making a centerpiece.

Calling for some butter, with nimble fingers and the skill of a practiced sculptor, in a short time the little scullion molded the figure of a crouching lion. So perfect in proportion, so spirited and full of life in every detail, was this marvelous butter lion that it elicited a chorus of admiration from the delighted guests, who were eager to know who the great sculptor was who had deigned to expend his genius on such perishable material. Signor Falieri, unable to gratify their curiosity, sent for his head servant, who gave them the history of the centerpiece. Antonio was immediately summoned to the banquet hall, where he blushingly received the praises and congratulations of all present, and the promise of Signer Falieri to become his patron, and thus enable him to achieve fame as a sculptor.

Such, according to some biographers, was the turning point in the career of Antonio Canova, who, from a peasant lad, born in the little Venetian village of Possagno, rose to be the most illustrious sculptor of his age.

Whether or not the story be true, it is certain that when the boy was in his thirteenth year, Signer Falieri placed him in the studio of Toretto, a Venetian sculptor, then living near Asola. But it is equally certain that the fame which crowned Canova's manhood, the title of Marquis of Ischia, the decorations and honors so liberally bestowed upon him by the ruler of the Vatican, kings, princes, and emperors, were all the fruits of his ceaseless industry, high ideals, and unfailing enthusiasm.

The little Antonio began to draw almost as soon as he could hold a pencil, and the gown of the dear old grandmother who so tenderly loved him, and was so tenderly loved in return, often bore the marks of baby fingers fresh from modeling in clay.

Antonio's father having died when the child was but three years old, his grandfather, Pisano, hoped that he would succeed him as village stonecutter and sculptor. Delicate though the little fellow had been from birth, at nine years of age he was laboring, as far as his strength would permit, in Pisano's workshop. But in the evening, after the work of the day was done, with pencil or clay he tried to give expression to the poetic fancies he had imbibed from the ballads and legends of his native hills, crooned to him in infancy by his grandmother.

Under Toretto his genius developed so rapidly that the sculptor spoke of one of his creations as "a truly marvelous production." He was then only thirteen. Later we find him in Venice, studying and working with ever increasing zeal. Though Signor Falieri would have been only too glad to supply the youth's needs, he was too proud to be dependent on others. Speaking of this time, he says: "I labored for a mere pittance, but it was sufficient. It was the fruit of my own resolution, and, as I then flattered myself, the foretaste of more honorable rewards, for I never thought of wealth."

Too poor to hire a workshop or studio, through the kindness of the monks of St. Stefano, he was given a cell in a vacant monastery, and here, at the age of sixteen, he started business as a sculptor on his own account.

Before he was twenty, the youth had become a master of anatomy, which he declared was "the secret of the art," was thoroughly versed in literature, languages, history, poetry, mythology,—everything that could help to make him the greatest sculptor of his age,—and had, even then, produced works of surpassing merit.

Effort to do better was the motto of his life, and he never permitted a day to pass without making some advance in his profession. Though often too poor to buy the marble in which to embody his conceptions, he for many years lived up to a resolution made about this time, never to close his eyes at night without having produced some design.

What wonder that at twenty-five this noble youth, whose incessant toil had perfected genius, was the marvel of his age! What wonder that his famous group, Theseus vanquishing the Minotaur, elicited the enthusiastic admiration of the most noted art critics of Rome! What wonder that the little peasant boy, who had first opened his eyes, in 1757, in a mud cabin, closed them at last, in 1822, in a marble palace, crowned with all of fame and honor and wealth the world could give! But better still, he was loved and enshrined in the hearts of the people, as a friend of the poor, a patron of struggling merit, a man in whom nobility of character overtopped even the genius of the artist.

***

FRANKLIN'S LESSON ON TIME VALUE

> Dost thou love life? Then, do not squander time, for that is the stuff life is made of!—FRANKLIN.

Franklin not only understood the value of time, but he put a price upon it that made others appreciate its worth.

A customer who came one day to his little bookstore in Philadelphia, not being satisfied with the price demanded by the clerk for the book he wished to purchase, asked for the proprietor. "Mr. Franklin is very busy just now in the press room," replied the clerk. The man, however, who had already spent an hour aimlessly turning over books, insisted on seeing him. In answer to the clerk's summons, Mr. Franklin hurried out from the newspaper establishment at the back of the store.

"What is the lowest price you can take for this book, sir?" asked the leisurely customer, holding up the volume. "One dollar and a quarter," was the prompt reply. "A dollar and a quarter! Why, your clerk asked me only a dollar just now." "True," said Franklin, "and I could have better afforded to take a dollar than to leave my work."

The man, who seemed to be in doubt as to whether Mr. Franklin was in earnest, said jokingly, "Well, come now, tell me your lowest price for this book." "One dollar and a half," was the grave reply. "A dollar and a half! Why, you just offered it for a dollar and a quarter." "Yes, and I could have better taken that price then than a dollar and a half now."

Without another word, the crestfallen purchaser laid the money on the counter and left the store. He had learned not only that he who squanders his own time is foolish, but that he who wastes the time of others is a thief.

***

FROM STORE BOY TO MILLIONAIRE

"But I am only nineteen years old, Mr. Riggs," and the speaker looked questioningly into the eyes of his companion, as if he doubted his seriousness in asking him to become a partner in his business.

Mr. Riggs was not joking, however, and he met George Peabody's perplexed gaze smilingly, as he replied: "That is no objection. If you are willing to go in with me and put your labor against my capital, I shall be well satisfied."

This was the turning point in a life which was to leave its impress on two of the world's greatest nations. And what were the experiences that led to it? They were utterly commonplace, and in some respects such as fall to the lot of many country boys to-day.

At eleven the lad was obliged to earn his own living. At that time (1806), his native town, Danvers, Massachusetts, presented few opportunities to the ambitious. He took the best that offered—a position as store boy in the village grocer's.

Four years of faithful work and constant effort at self-culture followed. He was now fifteen. His ambition was growing. He must seek a wider field. Another year passed, and then came the longed-for opening. Joyfully the youth set out for his brother's store, in Newburyport, Massachusetts. Here he felt he would have a better chance. But disappointment and disaster were lurking round the corner. Soon after he had taken up his new duties, the store was burned to the ground.

In the meantime, his father had died, and his mother, whom he idolized, needed his help more than ever. Penniless and out of work, but not disheartened, he immediately looked about for another position. Gladly he accepted an offer to work in his uncle's dry goods store in Georgetown, D.C., and here we find him, two years later, at the time when Mr. Riggs made his flattering proposition.

Did influence, a "pull," or financial considerations have anything to do with the merchant's choice of a partner? Nothing whatever. The young man had no money and no "pull," save what his character had made for him. His agreeable personality had won him many friends and his uncle much additional trade. His business qualities had gained him an enviable reputation. "His tact," says Sarah K. Bolton, "was unusual. He never wounded the feelings of a buyer of goods, never tried him with unnecessary talk, never seemed impatient, and was punctual to the minute."

That Mr. Riggs had made no mistake in choosing his partner, the rapid growth of his business conclusively proved. About a year after the partnership had been formed, the firm moved to Baltimore. So well did the business flourish in Baltimore that within seven years the partners had established branch houses in New York and Philadelphia. Finally Mr. Riggs decided to retire, and Peabody, who was then but thirty-five, found himself at the head of the business.

London, which he had visited several times, now attracted him. It offered great possibilities for banking. He went there, studied finance, established a banking business, and thenceforth made London his headquarters.

Wealth began to pour in upon him in a golden stream. But, although he had worked steadily for this, it was not for personal ends. He never married, and, to the end, lived simply and unostentatiously. Through the long years of patient work a great purpose had been shaping his life. Daily he had prayed that God might give him means wherewith to help his fellow-men. His prayer was being answered in overflowing measure.

Business interests constrained him to spend the latter half of his life in London; but absence only deepened his love for his own country. All that great wealth could do to advance the welfare and prestige of the

United States was done by the millionaire philanthropist. But above all else, he tried to bring within the reach of poor children that which was denied himself,—a school education.

The Peabody Institute in his native town, with its free library and free course of lectures; the Institute, Academy of Music, and Art Gallery of Baltimore; the Museum of Natural History at Yale University; the Museum of Archaeology and Ethnology at Harvard University; the Peabody Academy of Science at Salem, Massachusetts, besides large contributions every year to libraries and other educational and philanthropic institutions all over the country, bear witness to his love for humanity.

Surpassing all this, however, was his establishment of the Peabody fund of three million dollars for the education of the freed slaves of the South, and for the equally needy poor of the white race.

An equal amount had been previously devoted to the better housing of the London poor. A dream almost too good to come true it seemed to the toilers in the great city's slums, when they found their filthy, unhealthy tenements replaced by clean, wholesome dwellings, well supplied with air and sunlight and all modern conveniences and comforts. London presented its generous benefactor with the freedom of the city; a bronze statue was erected in his honor, and Queen Victoria, who would fain have loaded him with titles and honors,—all of which he respectfully declined,—declared his act to be "wholly without parallel." A beautiful miniature portrait of her Majesty, which she caused to be specially made for him, and a letter written by her own hand, were the only gifts he would accept.

Gloriously had his great purpose been fulfilled. He who began life as a poor boy had given to the furtherance of education and for the benefit of the poor in various ways the sum of nine million dollars. The remaining four million dollars of his fortune was divided among his relatives.

England loved and honored him even as his own country did; and when he died in London, November 4, 1869, she offered him a resting place among her immortals in Westminster Abbey. His last wish, however, was fulfilled, and he was laid beside his mother in his native land.

His legacies to humanity are doing their splendid work to-day as they have done in the past, and as they will continue to do in the future, enabling multitudes of aspiring souls to reach heights which but for him they never could have attained. These words of his, too, spoken on the occasion of the dedication of his gift to Danvers,—its free Institute,—will serve for ages as a bugle call to all youths who are anxious to make the most of themselves, and, like him, to give of their best to the world:—

"Though Providence has granted me an unvaried and unusual success in the pursuit of fortune in other lands," he said, "I am still in heart the humble boy who left yonder unpretending dwelling many, very many years ago. ... There is not a youth within the sound of my voice whose early opportunities and advantages are not very much greater than were my own; and I have since achieved nothing that is impossible to the most humble boy among you. Bear in mind, that, to be truly great, it is not necessary that you should gain wealth and importance. Steadfast and undeviating truth, fearless and straightforward integrity, and an honor ever unsullied by an unworthy word or action, make their possessor greater than worldly success or prosperity. These qualities constitute greatness."

***

“I WILL PAINT OR DIE!”

HOW A POOR, UNTAUGHT FARMER’S BOY BECAME AN ARTIST

“I will paint or die!” So stoutly resolved a poor, friendless boy, on a far-away Ohio farm, amid surroundings calculated to quench rather than to foster ambition. He knew not how his object was to be accomplished, for genius is never fettered by details. He only knew that he would be an artist. That settled it. He had never seen a work of art, or read or heard anything on the subject. It was his soul’s voice alone that spoke, and “the soul’s emphasis is always right.”

Left an orphan at the age of eleven, the boy agreed to work on his uncle’s farm for a term of five years for the munificent sum of ten dollars per annum, the total amount of which he was to receive at the end of the five years. The little fellow struggled bravely along with the laborious farm work, never for a moment losing sight of his ideal, and profiting as he could by the few months’ schooling snatched from the duties of the farm during the winter.

Toward the close of his five years’ service a great event happened. There came to the neighborhood an artist from Washington,—Mr. Uhl, whom he overheard by chance speaking on the subject of art. His words transformed the dream in the youth’s soul to a living purpose, and it was then he resolved that he would “paint or die,” and that he would go to Washington and study under Mr. Uhl.

On his release from the farm he started for Washington, with a coarse outfit packed away in a shabby little trunk, and a few dollars in his pocket. With the trustfulness of extreme youth, and in ignorance of a great world, he expected to get work that would enable him to live, and, at the same time, find leisure for the pursuit of his real life work. He immediately sought Mr. Uhl, who, with great generosity, offered to teach him without charge.

Then began the weary search for work in a large city already overcrowded with applicants. In his earnestness and eagerness the youth went from house to house asking for any kind of work "that would enable him to study art." But it was all in vain, and to save himself from starvation he was at length forced to accept the position of a day laborer, crushing stones for street paving. Yet he hoped to study painting when his day's work was done!

Mr. Uhl was at this time engaged in painting the portraits of Mrs. Frances Hodgson Burnett's sons. In the course of conversation with Mrs. Burnett, he spoke of the heroic struggle the youth was making. The author's heart was touched by the pathetic story. She at once wrote a check for one hundred dollars, and handed it to Mr. Uhl, for his protege. With that rare delicacy of feeling which marks all beautiful souls, Mrs. Burnett did not wish to embarrass the struggler by the necessity of thanking her. "Do not let him even write to me," she said to Mr. Uhl. "Simply say to him that I shall sail for Europe in a few days, and this is to give him a chance to work at the thing he cares for so much. It will at least give him a start."

In the throbbing life of the crowded city one heart beat high with hope and happiness that night. A youth lay awake until morning, too bewildered with gratitude and amazement to comprehend the meaning of the good fortune which had come to him. Who could his benefactor be?

Three years later, at the annual exhibition of Washington artists, Mrs. Burnett stood before a remarkably vivid portrait. Addressing the artist in charge of the exhibition, she said: "That seems to me very strong. It looks as if it must be a realistic likeness. Who did it?"

"I am so glad you like it. It was painted by your protege, Mrs. Burnett."

"My protege! My protege! Whom do you mean?"

"Why, the young man you saved from despair three years ago. Don't you remember young W——?"

"W——?" queried Mrs. Burnett.

"The young man whose story Mr. Uhl told you."

Mrs. Burnett then inquired if the portrait was for sale. When informed that the picture was an order and not for sale, she asked if there was anything else of Mr. W——'s on exhibition. She was conducted to a striking picture of a turbaned head, which was pointed out as another of Mr. W——'s works.

"How much does he ask for it?"

"A hundred and fifty dollars."

"Put 'sold' upon it, and when Mr. W—— comes, tell him his friend has bought his picture," said Mrs. Burnett.

On her return home Mrs. Burnett made out a check, which she inclosed in a letter to the young painter. It was mailed simultaneously with a letter from her protege, who had but just heard of her return from Europe, in which he begged her to accept, as a slight expression of his gratitude, the picture she had just purchased. The turbaned head now adorns the hall of Mrs. Burnett's house in Washington.

"I do not understand it even to-day," declares Mr. W——. "I knew nothing of Mrs. Burnett, nor she of me. Why did she do it? I only know that that hundred dollars was worth more to me then than fifty thousand in gold would be now. I lived upon it a whole year, and it put me on my feet."

Mr. W—— is a successful artist, now favorably known in his own country and in England for the strength and promise of his work.

***

THE CALL THAT SPEAKS IN THE BLOOD

Nature took the measure of little Tommy Edwards for a round hole, but his parents, teachers, and all with whom his childhood was cast, got it into their heads that Tommy was certainly intended for a square hole. So, with the best intentions in the world,—but oh, such woeful ignorance!—they tortured the poor little fellow and crippled him for life by trying to fit him to their pattern instead of that designed for him by the all-wise Mother.

Mother Nature called to Tommy to go into the woods and fields, to wade through the brooks, and make friends with all the living things she had placed there,—tadpoles, beetles, frogs, crabs, mice, rats, spiders, bugs,—everything that had life. Willingly, lovingly did the little lad obey, but only to be whipped and scolded by good Mother Edwards when he let loose in her kitchen the precious treasures which he had collected in his rambles.

It was provoking to have rats, mice, toads, bugs, and all sorts of creepy things sent sprawling over one's clean kitchen floor. But the pity of it was that Mrs. Edwards did not understand her boy, and thought the only cure for what she deemed his mischievous propensity as whipping. So Tommy was whipped and scolded, and scolded and whipped, which, however, did not in the least abate his love for Nature.

Driven to desperation, his mother bethought her of a plan. She would make the boy prisoner and see if this would tame him. With a stout rope she tied him by the leg to a table, and shut him in a room alone. But no sooner was the door closed than he dragged himself and the table to the fireplace, and, at the risk of setting himself and the house on fire, burned the rope which bound him, and made his escape into the woods to collect new specimens.

And yet his parents did not understand. It was time, however, to send him to school. They would see what the schoolmaster would do for him. But the schoolmaster was as blind as the parents, and Tommy's doom was sealed, when one morning, while the school was at prayers, a jackdaw poked its head out of his pocket and began to caw.

His next teacher misunderstood, whipped, and bore with him until one day nearly every boy in the school found a horse-leech wriggling up his leg, trying to suck his blood. This ended his second school experience.

He was given a third trial, but with no better results than before. Things went on in the usual way until a centipede was discovered in another boy's desk. Although in this case Tommy was innocent of any knowledge of the intruder, he was found guilty, whipped, and sent home with the message, "Go and tell your father to get you on board a man-of-war, as that is the best school for irreclaimables such as you."

His school life thus ended, he was apprenticed to a shoemaker, and thenceforth made his living at the bench. But every spare moment was given to the work which was meat and drink, life itself, to him.

In his manhood, to enable him to classify the minute and copious knowledge of birds, beasts, and insects which he had been gathering since childhood, with great labor and patience he learned how to read and write. Later, realizing how his lack of education hampered him, he endeavored to secure the means to enable him to study to better advantage, and sold for twenty pounds sterling a very large number of valuable specimens. He tried to get employment as a naturalist, and, but for his poor reading and writing, would have succeeded.

Poor little Scotch laddie! Had his parents or teachers understood him, he might have been as great a naturalist as Agassiz, and his life instead of being dwarfed and crippled, would have been a joy to himself and an incalculable benefit to the world.

***

WASHINGTON'S YOUTHFUL HEROISM

"No great deed is done
By falterers who ask for certainty."

"God will give you a reward," solemnly spoke the grateful mother, as she received from the arms of the brave youth the child he had risked his life to save. As if her lips were touched with the spirit of prophecy, she continued, "He will do great things for you in return for this day's work, and the blessings of thousands besides mine will attend you."

The ear of George Washington was ever open to the cry of distress; his sympathy and aid were ever at the service of those who needed them. One calm, sunny day, in the spring of 1750, he was dining with other surveyors in a forest in Virginia. Suddenly the stillness of the forest was startled by the piercing shriek of a woman. Washington instantly sprang to his feet and hurried to the woman's assistance.

"My boy, my boy,—oh, my poor boy is drowning, and they will not let me go," screamed the frantic mother, as she tried to escape from the detaining hands which withheld her from jumping into the rapids. "Oh, sir!" she implored, as she caught sight of the manly youth of eighteen, whose presence even then inspired confidence; "Oh, sir, you will surely do something for me!"

For an instant Washington measured the rocks and the whirling currents with a comprehensive look, and then, throwing off his coat, plunged into the roaring rapids where he had caught a glimpse of the drowning boy. With stout heart and steady hand he struggled against the seething mass of waters which threatened every moment to engulf or dash him to pieces against the sharp-pointed rocks which lay concealed beneath.

Three times he had almost succeeded in grasping the child's dress, when the force of the current drove him back. Then he gathered himself together for one last effort. Just as the child was about to escape him forever and be shot over the falls into the whirlpool below, he clutched him. The spectators on the bank cried out in horror. They gave both up for lost. But Washington seemed to lead a charmed life, and the cry of horror was changed to one of joy when, still holding the child, he emerged lower down from the vortex of waters.

Striking out for a low place in the bank, within a few minutes he reached the shore with his burden. Then amid the acclamations of those who had witnessed his heroism, and the blessings of the overjoyed mother, Washington placed the unconscious, but still living, child in her arms.

***

A COW HIS CAPITAL

A cow! Now, of all things in the world; of what use was a cow to an ambitious boy who wanted to go to college? Yet a cow, and nothing more, was the capital, the entire stock in trade, of an aspiring farmer boy who felt within him a call to another kind of life than that his father led.

This youth, who was yet in his teens, next to his father and mother, loved a book better than anything else in the world, and his great ambition was to go to college, to become a "scholar." Whether he followed the plow, or tossed hay under a burning July sun, or chopped wood, while his blood tingled from the combined effects of exercise and the keen December wind, his thoughts were ever fixed on the problem, "How can I go to college?"

His parents were poor, and, while they could give him a comfortable support as long as he worked on the farm with them, they could not afford to send him to college. But if they could not give him any material aid, they gave him all their sympathy, which kept the fire of his resolution burning at white heat.

There is some subtle communication between the mind and the spiritual forces of achievement which renders it impossible for one to think for any great length of time on a tangled problem, without a method for its untanglement being suggested. So, one evening, while driving the cows home to be milked, the thought flashed across the brain of the would-be student: "If I can't have anything else for capital, why can't I have a cow? I could do something with it, I am sure, and to college I MUST go, come what will." Courage is more than half the battle. Decision and Energy are its captains, and, when these three are united, victory is sure. The problem of going to college was already more than half solved.

Our youthful farmer did not let his thought grow cold. Hurrying at once to his father, he said, "If you will give me a cow, I shall feel free, with your permission, to go forth and see what I can do for myself in the world." The father, agreeing to the proposition, which seemed to him a practical one, replied heartily, "My son, you shall have the best milch cow I own."

Followed by the prayers and blessings of his parents, the youth started from home, driving his cow before him, his destination being a certain academy between seventy-five and one hundred miles distant.

Very soon he experienced the truth of the old adage that "Heaven helps those who help themselves." At the end of his first day's journey, when he sought a night's lodging for himself and accommodation for his cow in return for her milk, he met with unexpected kindness. The good people to whom he applied not only refused to take anything from him, but gave him bread to eat with his milk, and his cow a comfortable barn to lie in, with all the hay she could eat.

During the entire length of his journey, he met with equal kindness and consideration at the hands of all those with whom he came in contact; and, when he reached the academy, the principal and his wife were so pleased with his frank, modest, yet self-confident bearing, that they at once adopted himself and his cow into the family. He worked for his board, and the cow ungrudgingly gave her milk for the general good.

In due time the youth was graduated with honors from the academy. He was then ready to enter college, but had no money. The kind-hearted principal of the academy and his wife again came to his aid and helped him out of the difficulty by purchasing his cow. The money thus obtained enabled him to take the next step forward. He bade his good friends farewell, and the same year entered college. For four years he worked steadily with hand and brain. In spite of the hard work they were happy years, and at their close the persevering student had won, in addition to his classical degree, many new friends and well-wishers. His next step was to take a theological course in another institution. When he had finished the course, he was called to be principal of the academy to which honest ambition first led him with his cow.

Years afterward a learned professor of Hebrew, and the author of a scholarly "Commentary," cheered and encouraged many a struggling youth by relating the story of his own experiences from the time when he, a simple rustic, had started for college with naught but a cow as capital.

This story was first related to the writer by the late Frances E. Willard, who vouched for its truth.

***

THE BOY WHO SAID "I MUST"

Farther back than the memory of the grandfathers and grandmothers of some of my young readers can go, there lived in a historic town in Massachusetts a brave little lad who loved books and study more than toys or games, or play of any kind. The dearest wish of his heart was to be able to go to school every day, like more fortunate boys and girls, so that, when he should grow up to be a man, he might be well educated and fitted to do some grand work in the world. But his help was needed at home, and, young as he was, he began then to learn the lessons of unselfishness and duty. It was hard, wasn't it, for a little fellow only eight years old to have to leave off going to school and settle down to work on a farm? Many young folks at his age think they are very badly treated if they are not permitted to have some toy or story book, or other thing on which they have set their hearts; and older boys and girls, too, are apt to pout and frown if their whims are not gratified. But Theodore's parents were very poor, and could not even indulge his longing to go to school.

Did he give up his dreams of being a great man? Not a bit of it. He did not even cry or utter a complaint, but manfully resolved that he would do everything he could "to help father," and then, "when winter comes," he thought, "I shall be able to go to school again." Bravely the little fellow toiled through the beautiful springtide, though his wistful glances were often turned in the direction of the schoolhouse. But he resolutely bent to his work and renewed his resolve that he would be educated. As spring deepened into summer, the work on the farm grew harder and harder, but Theodore rejoiced that the flight of each season brought winter nearer.

At length autumn had vanished; the fruits of the spring and summer's toil had been gathered; the boy was free to go to his beloved studies again. And oh, how he reveled in the few books at his command in the village school! How eagerly he trudged across the fields, morning after morning, to the schoolhouse, where he always held first place in his class! Blustering winds and fierce snowstorms had no terrors for the ardent student. His only sorrow was that winter was all too short, and the days freighted with the happiness of regular study slipped all too quickly by. But the kind-hearted schoolmaster lent him books, so that, when spring came round again, and the boy had to go back to work, he could pore over them in his odd moments of relaxation. As he patiently plodded along, guiding the plow over the rough earth, he recited the lessons he had learned during the brief winter season, and after dinner, while the others rested awhile from their labors, Theodore eagerly turned the pages of one of his borrowed books, from which he drank in deep draughts of delight and knowledge. Early in the summer mornings, before the regular work began, and late in the evening, when the day's tasks had all been done, he read and re-read his treasured volumes until he knew them from cover to cover.

Then he was confronted with a difficulty. He had begun to study Latin, but found it impossible to get along without a dictionary. "What shall I do?" he thought; "there is no one from whom I can borrow a Latin dictionary, and I cannot ask father to buy me one, because he cannot afford it. But I MUST have it." That "must" settled the question. Three quarters of a century ago, book stores were few and books very costly. Boys and girls who have free access to libraries and reading rooms, and can buy the best works of great authors, sometimes for a few cents, can hardly imagine the difficulties which beset the little farmer boy in trying to get the book he wanted.

Did he get the dictionary? Oh, yes. You remember he had said, "I must." After thinking and thinking how he could get the money to buy it, a bright idea flashed across his mind. The bushes in the fields about the farm seemed waiting for some one to pick the ripe whortle-berries. "Why," thought he, "can't I gather and sell enough to buy my dictionary?" The next morning, before any one else in the farmhouse was astir, Theodore was moving rapidly through the bushes, picking, picking, picking, with unwearied fingers, the shining berries, every one of which was of greater value in his eyes than a penny would be to some of you.

At last, after picking and selling several bushels of ripe berries, he had enough money to buy the coveted dictionary. Oh, what a joy it was to possess a book that had been purchased with his own money! How it thrilled the boy and quickened his ambition to renewed efforts! "Well done, my boy! But, Theodore, I cannot afford to keep you there."

"Well, father," replied the youth, "but I am not going to study there; I shall study at home at odd times, and thus prepare myself for a final examination, which will give me a diploma."

Theodore had just returned from Boston, and was telling his delighted father how he had spent the holiday which he had asked for in the morning. Starting out early from the farm, so as to reach Boston before the intense heat of the August day had set in, he cheerfully tramped the ten miles that lay between his home in Lexington and Harvard College, where he presented himself as a candidate for admission; and when the examinations were over, Theodore had the joy of hearing his name announced in the list of successful students. The youth had reached the goal which the boy of eight had dimly seen. And now, if you would learn how he worked and taught in a country school in order to earn the money to spend two years in college, and how the young man became one of the most eminent preachers in America, you must read a complete biography of Theodore Parker, the hero of this little story.

***

THE HIDDEN TREASURE

Long, long ago, in the shadowy past, Ali Hafed dwelt on the shores of the River Indus, in the ancient land of the Hindus. His beautiful cottage, set in the midst of fruit and flower gardens, looked from the mountain side on which it stood over the broad expanse of the noble river. Rich meadows, waving fields of grain, and the herds and flocks contentedly grazing on the pasture lands, testified to the thrift and prosperity of Ali Hafed. The love of a beautiful wife and a large family of light-hearted boys and girls made his home an earthly paradise. Healthy, wealthy, contented, rich in love and friendship, his cup of happiness seemed full to overflowing.

Happy and contented, as we have seen, was the good Ali Hafed, when one evening a learned priest of Buddha, journeying along the banks of the Indus, stopped for rest and refreshment at his home, where all wayfarers were hospitably welcomed and treated as honored guests.

After the evening meal, the farmer and his family, with the priest in their midst, gathered around the fireside, the chilly mountain air of the late autumn making a fire desirable. The disciple of Buddha entertained his kind hosts with various legends and myths, and last of all with the story of the creation.

He told his wondering listeners how in the beginning the solid earth on which they lived was not solid at all, but a mere bank of fog. "The Great Spirit," said he, "thrust his finger into the bank of fog and began slowly describing a circle in its midst, increasing the speed gradually until the fog went whirling round his finger so rapidly that it was transformed into a glowing ball of fire. Then the Creative Spirit hurled the fiery ball from his hand, and it shot through the universe, burning its way through other banks of fog and condensing them into rain, which fell in great floods, cooling the surface of the immense ball. Flames then bursting from the interior through the cooled outer crust, threw up the hills and mountain ranges, and made the beautiful fertile valleys. In the flood of rain that followed this fiery upheaval, the substance that cooled very quickly formed granite, that which cooled less rapidly became copper, the next in degree cooled down into silver, and the last became gold. But the most beautiful substance of all, the diamond, was formed by the first beams of sunlight condensed on the earth's surface.

"A drop of sunlight the size of my thumb," said the priest, holding up his hand, "is worth more than mines of gold. With one such drop," he continued, turning to Ali Hafed, "you could buy many farms like yours; with a handful you could buy a province, and with a mine of diamonds you could purchase a whole kingdom."

The company parted for the night, and Ali Hafed went to bed, but not to sleep. All night long he tossed restlessly from side to side, thinking, planning, scheming how he could secure some diamonds. The demon of discontent had entered his soul, and the blessings and advantages which he possessed in such abundance seemed as by some malicious magic to have utterly vanished. Although his wife and children loved him as before; although his farm, his orchards, his flocks, and herds were as real and prosperous as they had ever been, yet the last words of the priest, which kept ringing in his ears, turned his content into vague longings and blinded him to all that had hitherto made him happy.

Before dawn next morning the farmer, full of his purpose, was astir. Rousing the priest, he eagerly inquired if he could direct him to a mine of diamonds.

"A mine of diamonds!" echoed the astonished priest. "What do you, who already have so much to be grateful for, want with diamonds?"

"I wish to be rich and place my children on thrones."

"All you have to do, then," said the Buddhist, "is to go and search until you find them."

"But where shall I go?" questioned the infatuated man.

"Go anywhere," was the vague reply; "north, south, east, or west,—anywhere."

"But how shall I know the place?" asked the farmer.

"When you find a river running over white sands between high mountain ranges, in these white sands you will find diamonds. There are many such rivers and many mines of diamonds waiting to be discovered. All you have to do is to start out and go somewhere—" and he waved his hand—"away, away!"

Ali Hafed's mind was full made up. "I will no longer," he thought, "remain on a wretched farm, toiling day in and day out for a mere subsistence, when acres of diamonds—untold wealth—may be had by him who is bold enough to seek them."

He sold his farm for less than half its value. Then, after putting his young family under the care of a neighbor, he set out on his quest.

With high hopes and the coveted diamond mines beckoning in the far distance, Ali Hafed began his wanderings. During the first few weeks his spirits did not flag, nor did his feet grow weary. On, and on, he tramped until he came to the Mountains of the Moon, beyond the bounds of Arabia. Weeks stretched into months, and the wanderer often looked regretfully in the direction of his once happy home. Still no gleam of waters glinting over white sands greeted his eyes. But on he went, into Egypt, through Palestine, and other eastern lands, always looking for the treasure he still hoped to find. At last, after years of fruitless search, during which he had wandered north and south, east and west, hope left him. All his money was spent. He was starving and almost naked, and the diamonds—which had lured him away from all that made life dear—where were they? Poor Ali Hafed never knew. He died by the wayside, never dreaming that the wealth for which he had sacrificed happiness and life might have been his had he remained at home.

"Here is a diamond! here is a diamond! Has Ali Hafed returned?" shouted an excited voice.

The speaker, no other than our old acquaintance, the Buddhist priest, was standing in the same room where years before he had told poor Ali Hafed how the world was made, and where diamonds were to be found.

"No, Ali Hafed has not returned," quietly answered his successor. "Neither is that which you hold in your hand a diamond; it is but a pretty black pebble I picked up in my garden."

"I tell you," said the priest, excitedly, "this is a genuine diamond. I know one when I see it. Tell me how and where you found it?"

"One day," replied the farmer, slowly, "having led my camel into the garden to drink, I noticed, as he put his nose into the water, a sparkle of light coming from the white sand at the bottom of the clear stream. Stooping down, I picked up the black pebble you now hold, guided to it by that crystal eye in the center from which the light flashes so brilliantly."

"Why, thou simple one," cried the priest, "this is no common stone, but a gem of the purest water. Come, show me where thou didst find it."

Together they flew to the spot where the farmer had found the "pebble," and, turning over the white sands with eager fingers, they found, to their great delight, other stones even more valuable and beautiful than the first. Then they extended their search, and, so the Oriental story goes, "every shovelful of the old farm, as acre after acre was sifted over, revealed gems with which to decorate the crowns of emperors and moguls."

***

LOVE TAMED THE LION

I would not enter on my list of friends,
(Though graced with polished manners and fine sense,
Yet wanting sensibility), the man
Who needlessly sets foot upon a worm.

COWPER.

"Nero!" Crushed, baffled, blinded, and, like Samson, shorn of his strength, prostrate in his cage lay the great tawny monarch of the forest. Heedless of the curious crowds passing to and fro, he seemed deaf as well as blind to everything going on around him. Perhaps he was dreaming of the jungle. Perhaps he was longing to roam the wilds once more in his native strength. Perhaps memories of a happy past even in captivity stirred him. Perhaps—But what is this? What change has come o'er the spirit of his dreams? No one has touched him. Apparently, nothing has happened to arouse him. Only a woman's voice, soft, caressing, full of love, has uttered the name, "Nero." But there was magic in the sound. In an instant the huge animal was on his feet. Quivering with emotion, he rushed to the side of the cage from whence the voice proceeded, and threw himself against the bars with such violence that he fell back half stunned. As he fell he uttered the peculiar note of welcome with which, in happier days, he was wont to greet his loved and long-lost mistress.

Touched with the devotion of her dumb friend, Rosa Bonheur—for it was she who had spoken—released from bondage the faithful animal whom, years before, she had bought from a keeper who declared him untamable.

"In order to secure the affections of wild animals," said the great-hearted painter, "you must love them," and by love she had subdued the ferocious beast whom even the lion-tamers had given up as hopeless.

When about to travel for two years, it being impossible to take her pet with her, Mademoiselle Bonheur sold him to the Jardin des Plantes in Paris, where she found him on her return, totally blind, owing, it is said, to the ill treatment of the attendant.

Grieved beyond measure at the condition of poor Nero, she had him removed to her chateau, where everything was done for his comfort that love could suggest. Often in her leisure moments, when she had laid aside her painting garb, the artist would have him taken to her studio, where she would play with and fondle the enormous creature as if he were a kitten. And there, at last, he died happily, his great paws clinging fondly to the mistress who loved him so well, his sightless eyes turned upon her to the end, as if beseeching that she would not again leave him.

***

"THERE IS ROOM ENOUGH AT THE TOP"

These words ere uttered many years ago by a youth who had no other means by which to reach the top than work and will. They have since become the watchword of every poor boy whose ambition is backed by energy and a determination to make the most possible of himself.

The occasion on which Daniel Webster first said "There is room enough at the top," marked the turning point in his life. Had he not been animated at that time by an ambition to make the most of his talents, he might have remained forever in obscurity.

His father and other friends had secured for him the position of Clerk of the Court of Common Pleas, of Hillsborough County, New Hampshire. Daniel was studying law in the office of Mr. Christopher Gore, a distinguished Boston lawyer, and was about ready for his admission to the bar. The position offered him was worth fifteen hundred dollars a year. This seemed a fortune to the struggling student. He lay awake the whole night following the day on which he had heard the good news, planning what he would do for his father and mother, his brother Ezekiel, and his sisters. Next morning he hurried to the office to tell Mr. Gore of his good fortune.

"Well, my young friend," said the lawyer, when Daniel had told his story, "the gentlemen have been very kind to you; I am glad of it. You must thank them for it. You will write immediately, of course."

Webster explained that, since he must go to New Hampshire immediately, it would hardly be worth while to write. He could thank his good friends in person.

"Why," said Mr. Gore in great astonishment, "you don't mean to accept it, surely!"

The youth's high spirits were damped at once by his senior's manner. "The bare idea of not accepting it," he says, "so astounded me that I should have been glad to have found any hole to have hid myself in."

"Well," said Mr. Gore, seeing the disappointment his words had caused, "you must decide for yourself; but come, sit down and let us talk it over. The office is worth fifteen hundred a year, you say. Well, it never will be any more. Ten to one, if they find out it is so much, the fees will be reduced. You are appointed now by friends; others may fill their places who are of different opinions, and who have friends of their own to provide for. You will lose your place; or, supposing you to retain it, what are you but a clerk for life? And your prospects as a lawyer are good enough to encourage you to go on. Go on, and finish your studies; you are poor enough, but there are greater evils than poverty; live on no man's favor; what bread you do eat, let it be the bread of independence; pursue your profession, make yourself useful to your friends and a little formidable to your enemies, and you have nothing to fear."

How fortunate Webster as to have at this point in his career so wise and far-seeing a friend! His father, who had made many sacrifices to educate his boys, saw in the proffered clerkship a great opening for his favorite, Daniel. He never dreamed of the future that was to make him one of America's greatest orators and statesmen. At first he could not believe that the position which he had worked so hard to obtain was to be rejected.

"Daniel, Daniel," he said sorrowfully, "don't you mean to take that office?"

"No, indeed, father," was the reply, "I hope I can do much better than that. I mean to use my tongue in the courts, not my pen; to be an actor, not a register of other men's acts. I hope yet, sir, to astonish your honor in your own court by my professional attainments."

Judge Webster made no attempt to conceal his disappointment. He even tried to discourage his son by reminding him that there were already more lawyers than the country needed.

It was in answer to this objection that Daniel used the famous and oft-quoted words,—"There is room enough at the top."

"Well, my son," said the fond but doubting father, "your mother has always said you would come to something or nothing. She was not sure which; I think you are now about settling that doubt for her."

It was very painful to Daniel to disappoint his father, but his purpose was fixed, and nothing now could change it. He knew he had turned his face in the right direction, and though when he commenced to practice law he earned only about five or six hundred dollars a year, he never regretted the decision he had made. He aimed high, and he had his reward.

It is true now and forever, as Lowell says, that—

> "Not failure, but low aim, is crime."

***

THE UPLIFT OF A SLAVE BOY'S IDEAL

> Invincible determination, and a right nature, are the levers that move the world.—PORTER.

Born a slave, with the feelings and possibilities of a man, but with no rights above the beast of the field, Fred Douglass gave the world one of the most notable examples of man's power over circumstances.

He had no knowledge of his father, whom he had never seen. He had only a dim recollection of his mother, from whom he had been separated at birth. The poor slave mother used to walk twelve miles when her day's work was done, in order to get an occasional glimpse of her child. Then she had to walk back to the plantation on which she labored, so as to be in time to begin to work at dawn next morning.

Under the brutal discipline of the "Aunt Katy" who had charge of the slaves who were still too young to labor in the fields, he early began to realize the hardships of his lot, and to rebel against the state of bondage into which he had been born.

Often hungry, and clothed in hottest summer and coldest winter alike, in a coarse tow linen shirt, scarcely reaching to the knees, without a bed to lie on or a blanket to cover him, his only protection, no matter how cold the night, was an old corn bag, into which he thrust himself, leaving his feet exposed at one end, and his head at the other.

When about seven years old, he was transferred to new owners in Baltimore, where his kind-hearted mistress, who did not know that in doing so she was breaking the law, taught him the alphabet. He thus got possession of the key which was to unlock his bonds, and, young as he was, he knew it. It did not matter that his master, when he learned what had been done, forbade his wife to give the boy further instructions. He had already tasted of the fruit of the tree of knowledge. The prohibition was useless. Neither threats nor stripes nor chains could hold the awakened soul in bondage.

With infinite pains and patience, and by stealth, he enlarged upon his knowledge of the alphabet. An old copy of "Webster's Spelling Book," cast aside by his young master, as his greatest treasure. With the aid of a few good-natured white boys, who sometimes played with him in the streets, he quickly mastered its contents. Then he cast about for further means to satisfy his mental craving. How difficult it was for the poor, despised slave to do this, we learn from his own pathetic words. "I have gathered," he says, "scattered pages of the Bible from the filthy street gutters, and washed and dried them, that, in moments of leisure, I might get a word or two of wisdom from them."

Think of that, boys and girls of the twentieth century, with your day schools and evening schools, libraries, colleges, and universities,—picking reading material from the gutter and mastering it by stealth! Yet this boy grew up to be the friend and co-worker of Garrison and Phillips, the eloquent spokesman of his race, the honored guest of distinguished peers and commoners of England, one of the noblest examples of a self-made man that the world has ever seen.

Under equal hardships he learned to write. The boy's wits, sharpened instead of blunted by repression, saw opportunities where more favored children could see none. He gave himself his first writing lesson in his master's shipyard, by copying from the various pieces of timber the letters with which they had been marked by the carpenters, to show the different parts of the ship for which they were intended. He copied from posters on fences, from old copy books, from anything and everything he could get hold of. He practiced his new art on pavements and rails, and entered into contests in letter making with white boys, in order to add to his knowledge. "With playmates for my teachers," he says, "fences and pavements for my copy books, and chalk for my pen and ink, I learned to write."

While being "broken in" to field labor under the lash of the overseer, chained and imprisoned for the crime of attempting to escape from slavery, the spirit of the youth never quailed. He believed in himself, in his God-given powers, and he was determined to use them in freeing himself and his race.

How well he succeeded in the stupendous task to which he set himself while yet groping in the black night of bondage, with no human power outside of his own indomitable will to help him, his life work attests in language more enduring than "storied urn" or written history. A roll call of the world's great moral heroes would be incomplete without the name of the slave-born Douglass, who came on the stage of life to play the leading role of the Moses of his race in one of the saddest and, at the same time, most glorious eras of American history.

He was born in Talbot County, Maryland. The exact date of his birth is not known; but he himself thought it was in February, 1817. He died in Washington, D.C., February 20, 1895.

***

"TO THE FIRST ROBIN"

The air was keen and biting, and traces of snow still lingered on the ground and sparkled on the tree tops in the morning sun. But the happy, rosy-cheeked children, lately freed from the restraints of city life, who played in the old garden in Concord, Massachusetts, that bright spring morning many years ago, heeded not the biting wind or the lingering snow. As they raced up and down the paths, in and out among the trees, their cheeks took on a deeper glow, their eyes a brighter sparkle, while their shouts of merry laughter made the morning glad.

But stay, what is this? What has happened to check the laughter on their lips, and dim their bright eyes with tears? The little group, headed by Louisa, has suddenly come to a pause under a tree, where a wee robin, half dead with hunger and cold, has fallen from its perch.

"Poor, poor birdie!" exclaimed a chorus of pitying voices. "It is dead, poor little thing," said Anna. "No," said Louisa, the leader of the children in fun and works of mercy alike; "it is warm, and I can feel its heart beat." As she spoke, she gathered the tiny bundle of feathers to her bosom, and, heading the little procession, turned toward the house.

A warm nest was made for the foundling, and, with motherly care, the little Louisa May Alcott, then only eight years old, fed and nursed back to life the half-famished bird.

Before the feathered claimant on her mercy flew away to freedom, the future authoress, the "children's friend," who loved and pitied all helpless things, wrote her first poem, and called it "To the First Robin." It contained only these two stanzas:—

"Welcome, welcome, little stranger,
Fear no harm, and fear no danger,
We are glad to see you here,
For you sing, 'Sweet spring is near.'

"Now the white snow melts away,
Now the flowers blossom gay,
Come, dear bird, and build your nest,
For we love our robin best."

***

THE "WIZARD" AS AN EDITOR

Although he had only a few months' regular schooling, at ten Thomas Alva Edison had read and thought more than many youths of twenty. Gibbon's "Rome," Hume's "England," Sears's "History of the World," besides several books on chemistry,—a subject in which he was even then deeply interested,—were familiar friends. Yet he was not, by any means, a serious bookworm. On the contrary, he was as full of fun and mischief as any healthy boy of his age.

The little fellow's sunny face and pleasing manners made him a general favorite, and when circumstances forced him from the parent nest into the big bustling world at the age of twelve, he became the most popular train boy on the Grand Trunk Railroad in central Michigan, while his keen powers of observation and practical turn of mind made him the most successful. His ambition soared far beyond the selling of papers, song books, apples, and peanuts, and his business ability was such that he soon had three or four boys selling his wares on commission.

His interest in chemistry, however, had not abated, and his busy brain now urged him to try new fields. He exchanged some of his papers for retorts and other simple apparatus, bought a copy of Fiesenius's "Qualitative Analysis," and secured the use of an old baggage car as a laboratory. Here, surrounded by chemicals and experimenting apparatus, he spent some of the happiest hours of his life.

But even this was not a sufficient outlet for the energies of the budding inventor. Selling papers had naturally aroused his interest in printing and editing, and with Edison interest always manifested itself in action. In buying papers, he had, as usual, made use of his eyes, and, with the little knowledge of printing picked up in this way, he determined to start a printing press and edit a paper of his own.

He first purchased a quantity of old type from the Detroit Free Press. Then he put a printing press in the baggage car, which did duty as printing and editorial office as well as laboratory, and began his editorial labors. When the first copy of the Grand Trunk Herald was put on sale, it would be hard to find a happier boy than its owner was.

No matter that the youthful editor's "Associated Press" consisted of baggage men and brakemen, or that the literary matter contributed to the Grand Trunk Herald was chiefly railway gossip, with some general information of interest to passengers, the little three-cent sheet became very popular. Even the great London Times deigned to notice it, as the only journal in the world printed on a railway train.

But, successful as he was in his editorial venture, Edison's best love was given to chemistry and electricity, which latter subject he had begun to study with his usual ardor. And well it was for the world when the youth of sixteen gave up train and newspaper work, that no poverty, no difficulties, no ridicule, no "hard luck," none of the trials and obstacles he had to encounter in after life, had power to chill or discourage the genius of the master inventor of the nineteenth century.

***

HOW GOOD FORTUNE CAME TO PIERRE

Many years ago, in a shabby room in one of the poorest streets of London, a little golden-haired boy sat singing, in his sweet, childish voice, by the bedside of his sick mother. Though faint from hunger and oppressed with loneliness, he manfully forced back the tears that kept welling up into his blue eyes, and, for his mother's sake, tried to look bright and cheerful. But it was hard to be brave and strong while his dear mother was suffering for lack of the delicacies which he longed to provide for her, but could not. He had not tasted food all day himself. How he could drive away the gaunt, hungry wolf, Famine, that had come to take up its abode with them, was the thought that haunted him as he tried to sing a little song he himself had composed. He left his place by the invalid, who, lulled by his singing, had fallen into a light sleep. As he looked listlessly out of the window, he noticed a man putting up a large poster, which bore, in staring yellow letters, the announcement that Madame M——, one of the greatest singers that ever lived, was to sing in public that night.

"Oh, if I could only go!" thought little Pierre, his love of music for the moment making him forgetful of aught else. Suddenly his face brightened, and the light of a great resolve shone in his eyes. "I will try it," he said to himself; and, running lightly to a little stand that stood at the opposite end of the room, with trembling hands he took from a tiny box a roll of paper. With a wistful, loving glance at the sleeper, he stole from the room and hurried out into the street.

"Who did you say is waiting for me?" asked Madame M—— of her servant; "I am already worn out with company."

"It is only a very pretty little boy with yellow curls, who said that if he can just see you, he is sure you will not be sorry, and he will not keep you a moment."

"Oh, well, let him come," said the great singer, with a kindly smile, "I can never refuse children."

Timidly the child entered the luxurious apartment, and, bowing before the beautiful, stately woman, he began rapidly, lest his courage should fail him: "I came to see you because my mother is very sick, and we are too poor to get food and medicine. I thought, perhaps, that if you would sing my little song at some of your grand concerts, maybe some publisher would buy it for a small sum, and so I could get food and medicine for my mother."

Taking the little roll of paper which the boy held in his hand, the warm-hearted singer lightly hummed the air. Then, turning toward him, she asked, in amazement: "Did you compose it? you, a child! And the words, too?" Without waiting for a reply, she added quickly, "Would you like to come to my concert this evening?" The boy's face became radiant with delight at the thought of hearing the famous songstress, but a vision of his sick mother, lying alone in the poor, cheerless room, flitted across his mind, and he answered, with a choking in his throat:—

"Oh, yes; I should so love to go, but I couldn't leave my mother."

"I will send somebody to take care of your mother for the evening, and here is a crown with which you may go and get food and medicine. Here is also one of my tickets. Come to-night; that will admit you to a seat near me."

Overcome with joy, the child could scarcely express his gratitude to the gracious being who seemed to him like an angel from heaven. As he went out again into the crowded street, he seemed to tread on air. He bought some fruit and other little delicacies to tempt his mother's appetite, and while spreading out the feast of good things before her astonished gaze, with tears in his eyes, he told her of the kindness of the beautiful lady.

An hour later, tingling with expectation, Pierre set out for the concert. How like fairyland it all seemed! The color, the dazzling lights, the flashing gems and glistening silks of the richly dressed ladies bewildered him. Ah! could it be possible that the great artist who had been so kind to him would sing his little song before this brilliant audience? At length she came on the stage, bowing right and left in answer to the enthusiastic welcome which greeted her appearance.

A pause of expectancy followed. The boy held his breath and gazed spellbound at the radiant vision on whom all eyes were riveted. The orchestra struck the first notes of a plaintive melody, and the glorious voice of the great singer filled the vast hall, as the words of the sad little song of the child composer floated on the air. It was so simple, so touching, so full of exquisite pathos, that many were in tears before it was finished.

And little Pierre? There he sat, scarcely daring to move or breathe, fearing that the flowers, the lights, the music, should vanish, and he should wake up to find it all a dream. He was aroused from his trance by the tremendous burst of applause that rang through the house as the last note trembled away into silence. He started up. It was no dream. The greatest singer in Europe had sung his little song before a fashionable London audience. Almost dazed with happiness, he never knew how he reached his poor home; and when he related the incidents of the evening, his mother's delight nearly equaled his own. Nor was this the end.

Next day they were startled by a visit from Madame M——. After gently greeting the sick woman, while her hand played with Pierre's golden curls, she said: "Your little boy, Madame, has brought you a fortune. I was offered this morning, by the best publisher in London, 300 pounds for his little song; and after he has realized a certain amount from the sale, little Pierre here is to share the profits. Madame, thank God that your son has a gift from heaven." The grateful tears of the invalid and her visitor mingled, while the child knelt by his mother's bedside and prayed God to bless the kind lady who, in their time of sorrow and great need, had been to them as a savior.

The boy never forgot his noble benefactress, and years afterward, when the great singer lay dying, the beloved friend who smoothed her pillow and cheered and brightened her last moments—the rich, popular, and talented composer—was no other than our little Pierre.

***

"IF I REST, I RUST"

> "The heights by great men reached and kept
> Were not attained by sudden flight;
> But they, while their companions slept,
> Were toiling upward in the night."

The significant inscription found on an old key,—"If I rest, I rust,"—would be an excellent motto for those who are afflicted with the slightest taint of idleness. Even the industrious might adopt it with advantage to serve as a reminder that, if one allows his faculties to rest, like the iron in the unused key, they will soon show signs of rust, and, ultimately, cannot do the work required of them.

Those who would attain

> "The heights by great men reached and kept"

must keep their faculties burnished by constant use, so that they will unlock the doors of knowledge, the gates that guard the entrances to the professions, to science, art, literature, agriculture,—every department of human endeavor.

Industry keeps bright the key that opens the treasury of achievement. If Hugh Miller, after toiling all day in a quarry, had devoted his evenings to rest and recreation, he would never have become a famous geologist. The celebrated mathematician, Edmund Stone, would never have published a mathematical dictionary, never have found the key to the science of mathematics, if he had given his spare moments, snatched from the duties of a gardener, to idleness. Had the little Scotch lad, Ferguson, allowed the busy brain to go to sleep while he tended sheep on the hillside, instead of calculating the position of the stars by the help of a string of beads, he would never have become a famous astronomer.

"Labor vanquishes all,"—not in constant, spasmodic, or ill-directed labor, but faithful, unremitting, daily effort toward a well-directed purpose. Just as truly as eternal vigilance is the price of liberty, so is eternal industry the price of noble and enduring success.

> "Seize, then, the minutes as they pass;
> The woof of life is thought!
> Warm up the colors; let them glow
> With fire of fancy fraught."

***

A BOY WHO KNEW NOT FEAR

Richard Wagner, the great composer, weaves into one of his musical dramas a beautiful story about a youth named Siegfried, who did not know what fear was.

The story is a sort of fairy tale or myth,—something which has a deep meaning hidden in it, but which is not literally true.

We smile at the idea of a youth who never knew fear, who even as a little child had never been frightened by the imaginary terrors of night, the darkness of the forest, or the cries of the wild animals which inhabited it.

Yet it is actually true that there was born at Burnham Thorpe, Norfolk, England, on September 29, 1758, a boy who never knew what fear was. This boy's name was Horatio Nelson,—a name which his fearlessness, ambition, and patriotism made immortal.

Courage even to daring distinguished young Nelson from his boy companions. Many stories illustrating this quality are told of him.

On one occasion, when the future hero of England was but a mere child, while staying at his grandmother's, he wandered away from the house in search of birds' nests. When dinner time came and went and the boy did not return, his family became alarmed. They feared that he had been kidnapped by gypsies, or that some other mishap had befallen him. A thorough search was made for him in every direction. Just as the searchers were about to give up their quest, the truant was discovered sitting quietly by the side of a brook which he was unable to cross.

"I wonder, child," said his grandmother, "that hunger and fear did not drive you home."

"Fear! grand-mamma," exclaimed the boy; "I never saw fear. What is it?"

Horatio was a born leader, who never even in childhood shrank from a hazardous undertaking. This story of his school days shows how the spirit of leadership marked him before he had entered his teens.

In the garden attached to the boarding school at North Walsham, which he and his elder brother, William, attended, there grew a remarkably fine pear tree. The sight of this tree, loaded with fruit was, naturally, a very tempting one to the boys. The boldest among the older ones, however, dared not risk the consequences of helping themselves to the pears, which they knew were highly prized by the master of the school.

Horatio, who thought neither of the sin of stealing the schoolmaster's property, nor of the risk involved in the attempt, volunteered to secure the coveted pears.

He was let down in sheets from the bedroom window by his schoolmates, and, after gathering as much of the fruit as he could carry, returned with considerable difficulty. He then turned the pears over to the boys, not keeping one for himself.

"I only took them," he explained, "because the rest of you were afraid to venture."

The sense of honor of the future "Hero of the Nile" and of Trafalgar was as keen in boyhood as in later life.

One year, at the close of the Christmas holidays, he and his brother William set out on horseback to return to school. There had been a heavy fall of snow which made traveling very disagreeable, and William persuaded Horatio to go back home with him, saying that it was not safe to go on.

"If that be the case," said Rev. Mr. Nelson, thc father of the boys, when the matter was explained to him, "you certainly shall not go; but make another attempt, and I will leave it to your honor. If the road is dangerous, you may return; but remember, boys, I leave it to your honor."

The snow was really deep enough to be made an excuse for not going on, and William was for returning home a second time. Horatio, however, would not be persuaded again. "We must go on," he said; "remember, brother, it was left to our honor."

When only twelve years old, young Nelson's ambition urged him to try his fortune at sea. His uncle, Captain Maurice Suckling, commanded the Raisonnable, a ship of sixty-four guns, and the boy thought it would be good fortune, indeed, if he could get an opportunity to serve under him. "Do, William," he said to his brother, "write to my father, and tell him that I should like to go to sea with Uncle Maurice."

On hearing of his son's wishes, Mr. Nelson at once wrote to Captain Suckling. The latter wrote back without delay: "What has poor Horatio done, who is so weak, that he, above all the rest, should be sent to rough it out at sea? But let him come, and the first time we go into action, a cannon ball may knock off his head and provide for him at once."

This was not very encouraging for a delicate boy of twelve. But Horatio was not daunted. His father took him to London, and there put him into the stage coach for Chatham, where the Raisonnable was lying at anchor.

He arrived at Chatham during the temporary absence of his uncle, so that there was no friendly voice to greet him when he went on board the big ship. Homesick and heartsick, he passed some of the most miserable days of his life on the Raisonnable. The officers treated the sailors with a harshness bordering on cruelty. This treatment, of course, increased the natural roughness of the sailors; and, altogether, the conditions were such that Horatio's opinion of the Royal Navy was sadly altered.

But in spite of the separation from his brother William, who had been his schoolmate and constant companion, and all his other loved ones, the hardships he had to endure as a sailor boy among rough officers and rougher men, and his physical weakness, his courage did not fail him. He stuck bravely to his determination to be a sailor.

Later, the lad went on a voyage to the West Indies, in a merchant ship commanded by Mr. John Rathbone. During this voyage, his anxiety to rise in his profession and his keen powers of observation, which were constantly exercised, combined to make him a practical sailor.

After his return from the West Indies, his love of adventure was excited by the news that two ships—the Racehorse and the Carcass—were being fitted out for a voyage of discovery to the North Pole. Through the influence of Captain Suckling, he secured an appointment as coxswain, under Captain Lutwidge, who was second in command of the expedition.

All went well with the Racehorse and the Carcass until they neared the Polar regions. Then they were becalmed, surrounded with ice, and wedged in so that they could not move.

Young as Nelson was, he was put in command of one of the boats sent out to try to find a passage to the open water. While engaged in this work he was instrumental in saving the crew of another of the boats which had been attacked by walruses.

His most notable adventure during this Polar cruise, however, was a fight with a bear.

One night he stole away from his ship with a companion in pursuit of a bear. A fog which had been rising when they left the Carcass soon enveloped them. Between three and four o'clock in the morning, when the weather began to clear, they were sighted by Captain Lutwidge and his officers, at some distance from the ship, in conflict with a huge bear. The boys, who had been missed soon after they set out on their adventure, were at once signaled to return. Nelson's companion urged him to obey the signal, and, though their ammunition had given out, he longed to continue the fight.

"Never mind," he cried excitedly; "do but let me get a blow at this fellow with the butt end of my musket, and we shall have him."

Captain Lutwidge, seeing the boy's danger,—he being separated from the bear only by a narrow chasm in the ice,—fired a gun. This frightened the bear away. Nelson then returned to face the consequences of his disobedience.

He was severely reprimanded by his captain for "conduct so unworthy of the office he filled." When asked what motive he had in hunting a bear, he replied, still trembling from the excitement of the encounter, "Sir, I wished to kill the bear that I might carry the skin to my father."

The expedition finally worked its way out of the ice and sailed for home.

Horatio's next voyage was to the East Indies, aboard the Seahorse, one of the vessels of a squadron under the command of Sir Edward Hughes. His attention to duty attracted the notice of his senior officer, on whose recommendation he was rated as a midshipman.

After eighteen months in the trying climate of India, the youth's health gave way, and he was sent home in the Dolphin. His physical weakness affected his spirits. Gloom fastened upon him, and for a time he was very despondent about his future.

"I felt impressed," he says, "with an idea that I should never rise in my profession. My mind was staggered with a view of the difficulties I had to surmount and the little interest I possessed. I could discover no means of reaching the object of my ambition. After a long and gloomy revery in which I almost wished myself overboard, a sudden flow of patriotism was kindled within me and presented my king and my country as my patrons. My mind exulted in the idea. 'Well, then,' I exclaimed, 'I will be a hero, and, confiding in Providence, I will brave every danger!'"

In that hour Nelson leaped from boyhood to manhood. Thenceforth the purpose of his life never changed. From that time, as he often said afterward, "a radiant orb was suspended in his mind's eye, which urged him onward to renown."

His health improved very much during the homeward voyage, and he was soon able to resume duty again.

At nineteen he was made second lieutenant of the Lowestoffe; and at twenty he was commander of the Badger. Before he was twenty-one, owing largely to his courage and presence of mind in face of every danger, and his enthusiasm in his profession, "he had gained that mark," says his biographer, Southey, "which brought all the honors of the service within his reach."

Pleasing in his address and conversation, always kind and thoughtful in his treatment of the men and boys under him, Nelson was the best-loved man in the British navy,—nay, in all England.

When he was appointed to the command of the Boreas, a ship of twenty-eight guns, then bound for the Leeward Islands, he had thirty midshipmen under him. When any of them, at first, showed any timidity about going up the masts, he would say, by way of encouragement, "I am going a race to the masthead, and beg that I may meet you there." And again he would say cheerfully, that "any person was to be pitied who could fancy there was any danger, or even anything disagreeable, in the attempt."

"Your Excellency must excuse me for bringing one of my midshipmen with me," he said to the governor of Barbados, who had invited him to dine. "I make it a rule to introduce them to all the good company I can, as they have few to look up to besides myself during the time they are at sea." Was it any wonder that his "middies" almost worshiped him?

This thoughtfulness in small matters is always characteristic of truly great, large-souled men. Another distinguishing mark of Nelson's greatness was that he ruled by love rather than fear.

When, at the age of forty-seven, he fell mortally wounded at the battle of Trafalgar, all England was plunged into grief. The crowning victory of his life had been won, but his country was inconsolable for the loss of the noblest of her naval heroes.

"The greatest sea victory that the world had ever known was won," says W. Clark Russell, "but at such a cost, that there was no man throughout the British fleet—there was no man indeed in all England—but would have welcomed defeat sooner than have paid the price of this wonderful conquest."

The last words of the hero who had won some of the greatest of England's sea fights were, "Thank God, I have done my duty."

***

HOW STANLEY FOUND LIVINGSTONE

In the year 1866 David Livingstone, the great African explorer and missionary, started on his last journey to Africa. Three years passed away during which no word or sign from him had reached his friends. The whole civilized world became alarmed for his safety. It was feared that his interest in the savages in the interior of Africa had cost him his life.

Newspapers and clergymen in many lands were clamoring for a relief expedition to be sent out in search of him. Royal societies, scientific associations, and the British government were debating what steps should be taken to find him. But they were very slow in coming to any conclusion, and while they were weighing questions and discussing measures, an energetic American settled the matter offhand.

This was James Gordon Bennett, Jr., manager of the New York Herald and son of James Gordon Bennett, its editor and proprietor.

Mr. Bennett was in a position which brought him into contact with some of the cleverest and most enterprising young men of his day. From all those he knew he singled out Henry M. Stanley for the difficult and perilous task of finding Livingstone.

And who was this young man who was chosen to undertake a work which required the highest qualities of manhood to carry it to success?

Henry M. Stanley, whose baptismal name was John Rowlands, was born of poor parents in Wales, in 1840. Being left an orphan at the age of three, he was sent to the poorhouse in his native place. There he remained for ten years, and then shipped as a cabin boy in a vessel bound for America. Soon after his arrival in this country, he found employment in New Orleans with a merchant named Stanley. His intelligence, energy, and ambition won him so much favor with this gentleman that he adopted him as his son and gave him his name.

The elder Stanley died while Henry was still a youth. This threw him again upon his own resources, as he inherited nothing from his adopted father, who died without making a will. He next went to California to seek his fortune. He was not successful, however, and at twenty he was a soldier in the Civil War. When the war was over, he engaged himself as a correspondent to the New York Herald.

In this capacity he traveled extensively in the East, doing brilliant work for his paper. When England went to war with King Theodore of Abyssinia, he accompanied the English army to Abyssinia, and from thence wrote vivid descriptive letters to the Herald. The child whose early advantages were only such as a Welsh poorhouse afforded, was already, through his own unaided efforts, a leader in his profession. He was soon to become a leader in a larger sense.

At the time Mr. Bennett conceived the idea of sending an expedition in search of Livingstone, Stanley was in Spain. He had been sent there by the Herald to report the civil war then raging in that country. He thus describes the receipt of Mr. Bennett's message and the events immediately following:—

"I am in Madrid, fresh from the carnage at Valencia. At 10 A.M. Jacopo, at No.—Calle de la Cruz, hands me a telegram; on opening it I find it reads, 'Come to Paris on important business.' The telegram is from James Gordon Bennett, Jr., the young manager of the New York Herald.

"Down come my pictures from the walls of my apartments on the second floor; into my trunks go my books and souvenirs, my clothes are hastily collected, some half washed, some from the clothesline half dry, and after a couple of hours of hasty hard work my portmanteaus are strapped up and labeled for 'Paris.'"

It was late at night when Stanley arrived in Paris. "I went straight to the 'Grand Hotel,'" he says, "and knocked at the door of Mr. Bennett's room.

"'Come in,' I heard a voice say. Entering I found Mr. Bennett in bed.

"'Who are you?' he asked.

"'My name is Stanley,' I answered.

"'Ah, yes! sit down; I have important business on hand for you.

"'Where do you think Livingstone is?'

"'I really do not know, sir.'

"'Do you think he is alive?'

"'He may be, and he may not be,' I answered.

"'Well, I think he is alive, and that he can be found, and I am going to send you to find him.'

"'What!' said I, 'do you really think I can find Dr. Livingstone? Do you mean me to go to Central Africa?'

"'Yes, I mean that you shall go and find him wherever you may hear that he is.... Of course you will act according to your own plans and do what you think best—BUT FIND LIVINGSTONE.'"

The question of expense coming up, Mr. Bennett said: "Draw a thousand pounds now; and when you have gone through that, draw another thousand; and when that is spent, draw another thousand; and when you have finished that, draw another thousand, and so on; but, FIND LIVINGSTONE."

Stanley asked no questions, awaited no further instructions. The two men parted with a hearty hand clasp. "Good night, and God be with you," said Bennett.

"Good night, sir," returned Stanley. "What it is in the power of human nature to do I will do; and on such an errand as I go upon, God will be with me."

The young man immediately began the work of preparation for his great undertaking. This in itself was a task requiring more than ordinary judgment and foresight, but Stanley was equal to the occasion.

On January 6, 1871, he reached Zanzibar, an important native seaport on the east coast of Africa. Here the preparations for the journey were completed. Soon, with a train composed of one hundred and ninety men, twenty donkeys, and baggage amounting to about six tons, he started from this point for the interior of the continent.

Then began a journey the dangers and tediousness of which can hardly be described. Stanley and his men were often obliged to wade through swamps filled with alligators. Crawling on hands and knees, they forced their way through miles of tangled jungle, breathing in as they went the sickening odor of decaying vegetables. They were obliged to be continually on their guard against elephants, lions, hyenas, and other wild inhabitants of the jungle. Fierce as these were, however, they were no more to be dreaded than the savage tribes whom they sometimes encountered. Whenever they stopped to rest, they were tormented by flies, white ants, and reptiles, which crawled all over them.

For months they journeyed on under these conditions. The donkeys had died from drinking impure water, and some of the men had fallen victims to disease.

It was no wonder that the survivors of the expedition—all but Stanley—had grown disheartened. Half starved, wasted by sickness and hardships of all kinds, with bleeding feet and torn clothes, some of them became mutinous. Stanley's skill as a leader was taxed to the utmost. Alternately coaxing the faint-hearted and punishing the insubordinate, he continued to lead them on almost in spite of themselves.

So far they had heard nothing of Livingstone, nor had they any clew as to the direction in which they should go. There was no ray of light or hope to cheer them on their way, yet Stanley never for a moment thought of giving up the search.

Once, amid the terrors of the jungle, surrounded by savages and wild animals, with supplies almost exhausted, and the remnant of his followers in a despairing condition, the young explorer came near being discouraged.

But he would not give way to any feeling that might lessen his chances of success, and it was at this crisis he wrote in his journal:—

"No living man shall stop me—only death can prevent me. But death—not even this; I shall not die—I will not die—I cannot die! Something tells me I shall find him and—write it larger—FIND HIM, FIND HIM! Even the words are inspiring."

Soon after this a caravan passed and gave the expedition news which renewed hope: A white man, old, white haired, and sick, had just arrived at Ujiji.

Stanley and his followers pushed on until they came in sight of Ujiji. Then the order was given to "unfurl the flags and load the guns." Immediately the Stars and Stripes and the flag of Zanzibar were thrown to the breeze, and the report of fifty guns awakened the echoes. The noise startled the inhabitants of Ujiji. They came running in the direction of the sounds, and soon the expedition was surrounded by a crowd of friendly black men, who cried loudly, "YAMBO, YAMBO, BANA!" which signifies welcome.

"At this grand moment," says Stanley, "we do not think of the hundreds of miles we have marched, of the hundreds of hills that we have ascended and descended, of the many forests we have traversed, of the jungle and thickets that annoyed us, of the fervid salt plains that blistered our feet, of the hot suns that scorched us, nor the dangers and difficulties now happily surmounted.

"At last the sublime hour has arrived!—our dreams, our hopes and anticipations are now about to be realized! Our hearts and our feelings are with our eyes, as we peer into the palms and try to make out in which hut or house lives the white man with the gray beard we heard about on the Malagarazi."

When the uproar had ceased, a voice was heard saluting the leader of the expedition in English—"Good morning, sir."

"Startled at hearing this greeting in the midst of such a crowd of black people," says Stanley, "I turn sharply round in search of the man, and see him at my side, with the blackest of faces, but animated and joyous—a man dressed in a long white shirt, with a turban of American sheeting around his head, and I ask, 'Who the mischief are you?'

"'I am Susi, the servant of Dr. Livingstone,' said he, smiling, and showing a gleaming row of teeth.

"'What! Is Dr. Livingstone here?'

"'Yes, sir.'

"'In this village?'

"'Yes, sir.'

"'Are you sure?'

"'Sure, sure, sir. Why, I leave him just now.'

"'Susi, run, and tell the Doctor I am coming.'"

Susi ran like a madman to deliver the message. Stanley and his men followed more slowly. Soon they were gazing into the eyes of the man for news of whom the whole civilized world was waiting.

"My heart beat fast," says Stanley, "but I must not let my face betray my emotions, lest it shall detract from the dignity of a white man appearing under such extraordinary circumstances."

The young explorer longed to leap and shout for joy, but he controlled himself, and instead of embracing Livingstone as he would have liked to do, he grasped his hand, exclaiming, "I thank God, Doctor, that I have been permitted to see you."

"I feel grateful that I am here to welcome you," was the gentle reply.

All the dangers through which they had passed, all the privations they had endured were forgotten in the joy of this meeting. Doctor Livingstone's years of toil and suspense, during which he had heard nothing from the outside world; Stanley's awful experiences in the jungle, the fact that both men had almost exhausted their supplies; the terrors of open and hidden dangers from men and beasts, sickness, hope deferred, all were, for the moment, pushed out of mind. Later, each recounted his story to the other.

After a period of rest, the two joined forces and together explored and made plans for the future. Stanley tried to induce Livingstone to return with him. But in vain; the great missionary explorer would not lay down his work. He persevered, literally until death.

At last the hour of parting came. With the greatest reluctance Stanley gave his men the order, "Right about face." With a silent farewell, a grasp of the hands, and a look into each other's eyes which said more than words, the old man and the young man parted forever.

Livingstone's life work was almost done. Stanley was the man on whose shoulders his mantle was to fall. The great work he had accomplished in finding Livingstone was the beginning of his career as an African explorer.

After the death of Livingstone, Stanley determined to take up the explorer's unfinished work.

In 1874 he left England at the head of an expedition fitted out by the London Daily Telegraph and the New York Herald, and penetrated into the very heart of Africa.

He crossed the continent from shore to shore, overcoming on his march dangers and difficulties compared with which those encountered on his first journey sank into insignificance. He afterward gave an account of this expedition in his book entitled, "Darkest Africa."

Stanley had successfully accomplished one of the great works of the world. He had opened the way for commerce and Christianity into the vast interior of Africa, which, prior to his discoveries, had been marked on the map by a blank space, signifying that it was an unexplored and unknown country.

On his return the successful explorer found himself famous. Princes and scientific societies vied with one another in honoring him. King Edward VII of England, who was then Prince of Wales, sent him his personal congratulations; Humbert, the king of Italy, sent him his portrait; the khedive of Egypt decorated him with the grand commandership of the Order of the Medjidie; the Geographical Societies of London, Paris, Italy, and Marseilles sent him their gold medals; while in Berlin, Vienna, and many other large European cities, he was elected an honorary member of their most learned and most distinguished associations.

What pleased the explorer most of all, though, was the honor paid him by America. "The government of the United States," he says, "has crowned my success with its official approval, and the unanimous vote of thanks passed in both houses of the legislature has made me proud for life of the expedition and its achievements."

Honored to-day as the greatest explorer of his age, and esteemed alike for his scholarship and the immense services he has rendered mankind, Sir Henry Morton Stanley, the once friendless orphan lad whose only home was a Welsh poorhouse, may well be proud of the career he has carved out for himself.

***

THE NESTOR OF AMERICAN JOURNALISTS

"I heard that a neighbor three miles off, had borrowed from a still more distant neighbor, a book of great interest. I started off, barefoot, in the snow, to obtain the treasure. There were spots of bare ground, upon which I would stop to warm my feet. And there were also, along the road, occasional lengths of log fence from which the snow had melted, and upon which it was a luxury to walk. The book was at home, and the good people consented, upon my promise that it should be neither torn nor soiled, to lend it to me. In returning with the prize, I was too happy to think of the snow on my naked feet."

This little incident, related by Thurlow Weed himself, is a sample of the means by which he gained that knowledge and power which made him not only the "Nestor of American Journalists," but rendered him famous in national affairs as the "American Warwick" or "The King Maker."

There were no long happy years of schooling for this child of the "common people," whose father was a struggling teamster and farmer; no prelude of careless, laughing childhood before the stern duties of life began.

Thurlow Weed was born at Catskill, Greene County, New York, in 1797, a period in the history of our republic when there were very few educational opportunities for the children of the poor. "I cannot ascertain," he says, "how much schooling I got at Catskill, probably less than a year, certainly not a year and a half, and this was when I was not more than five or six years old."

At an early age Thurlow learned to bend circumstances to his will and, ground by poverty, shut in by limitations as he was, even while contributing by his earning to the slender resources of the family, he gathered knowledge and pleasure where many would have found but thorns and bitterness.

How simply he tells his story, as though his hardships and struggles were of no account, and how clearly the narrative mirrors the brave little fellow of ten!

"My first employment," he says, "was in sugar making, an occupation to which I became much attached. I now look with great pleasure upon the days and nights passed in the sap-bush. The want of shoes (which, as the snow was deep, was no small privation) was the only drawback upon my happiness. I used, however, to tie pieces of an old rag carpet around my feet, and got along pretty well, chopping wood and gathering up sap."

During this period he traveled, barefoot, to borrow books, wherever they could be found among the neighboring farmers. With his body in the sugar house, and his head thrust out of doors, "where the fat pine was blazing," the young enthusiast devoured with breathless interest a "History of the French Revolution," and the few other well-worn volumes which had been loaned him.

Later, after he left the farm, we see the future journalist working successively as cabin boy and deck hand on a Hudson River steamboat, and cheerfully sending home the few dollars he earned. While employed in this capacity, he earned his first "quarter" in New York by carrying a trunk for one of the passengers from the boat to a hotel on Broad Street.

But his boyish ambition was to be a journalist, and, after a year of seafaring life, he found his niche in the office of a small weekly newspaper, the Lynx, published at Onondaga Hollow, New York.

So, at fourteen, owing to his indomitable will and perseverance, which conquered the most formidable obstacles, Thurlow Weed started on the career in which, despite the rugged road he still had to travel, he·built up a noble character and won international fame.

***

THE MAN WITH AN IDEA

It is February, 1492. A poor man, with gray hair, disheartened and dejected, is going out of the gate from the beautiful Alhambra, in Granada, on a mule. Ever since he was a boy, he has been haunted with the idea that the earth is round. He has believed that the pieces of carved wood, picked up four hundred miles at sea, and the bodies of two men, unlike any other human beings known, found on the shores of Portugal, have drifted from unknown lands in the west. But his last hope of obtaining aid for a voyage of discovery has failed. King John of Portugal, under pretense of helping him, has secretly sent out an expedition of his own. His friends have abandoned him; he has begged bread; has drawn maps to keep him from starving, and lost his wife; his friends have called him crazy, and have forsaken him. The council of wise men, called by Ferdinand and Isabella, ridicule his theory of reaching the east by sailing west. "But the sun and moon are round," replies Columbus, "why not the earth?" "If the earth is a ball, what holds it up?" the wise men ask. "What holds the sun and moon up?" Columbus replies.

A learned doctor asks, "How can men walk with their heads hanging down, and their feet up, like flies on a ceiling?" "How can trees grow with their roots in the air?" "The water would run out of the ponds, and we should fall off," says another. "The doctrine is contrary to the Bible, which says, 'The heavens are stretched out like a tent.'" "Of course it is flat; it is rank heresy to say it is round."

He has waited seven long years. He has had his last interview, hoping to get assistance from Ferdinand and Isabella after they drive the Moors out of Spain. Isabella was almost persuaded, but finally refused. He is now old, his last hope has fled; the ambition of his life has failed. He hears a voice calling him. He looks back and sees an old friend pursuing him on a horse, and beckoning him to come back. He saw Columbus turn away from the Alhambra, disheartened, and he hastens to the queen and tells her what a great thing it would be, at a trifling expense, if what the sailor believes should prove true. "It shall be done," Isabella replies. "I will pledge my jewels to raise the money; call him back." Columbus turns back, and with him turns the world.

Three frail vessels, little larger than fishing boats, the Santa Maria, the Pinta, and the Nina, set sail from Palos, August 3, 1492, for an unknown land, upon untried seas; the sailors would not volunteer, but were forced to go by the king. Friends ridiculed them for following a crazy man to certain destruction, for they believed the sea beyond the Canaries was boiling hot. "What if the earth is round?" they said, "and you sail down the other side, how can you get back again? Can ships sail up hill?"

Only three days out, the Pinto's signal of distress is flying; she has broken her rudder. September 8 they discover a broken mast covered with seaweed floating in the sea. Terror seizes the sailors, but Columbus calms their fears with pictures of gold and precious stones of India. September 13, two hundred miles west of the Canaries, Columbus is horrified to find that the compass, his only guide, is failing him, and no longer points to the north star. No one had yet dreamed that the earth turns on its axis. The sailors are ready for mutiny, but Columbus tells them the north star is not exactly in the north. October 1 they are two thousand three hundred miles from land, though Columbus tells the sailors one thousand seven hundred. Columbus discovers a bush in the sea, with berries on it, and soon they see birds and a piece of carved wood. At sunset, the crew kneel upon the deck and chant the vesper hymn. It is sixty-seven days since they left Palos, and they have sailed nearly three thousand miles, only changing their course once. At ten o'clock at night they see a light ahead, but it vanishes. Two o'clock in the morning, October 12, Roderigo de Friana, on watch at the masthead of the Pinta, shouts, "Land! land! land!" The sailors are wild with joy, and throw themselves on their knees before Columbus, and ask forgiveness. They reach the shore, and the hero of the world's greatest expedition unfolds the flag of Spain and takes possession of the new world. Perhaps no greater honor was ever paid man than Columbus received on his return to Ferdinand and Isabella. Yet, after his second visit to the land he discovered, he was taken back to Spain in chains, and finally died in poverty and neglect; while a pickle dealer of Seville, who had never risen above second mate, on a fishing vessel, Amerigo Vespucci, gave his name to the new world. Amerigo's name was put on an old chart or sketch to indicate the point of land where he landed, five years after Columbus discovered the country, and this crept into print by accident.

***

"BERNARD OF THE TUILERIES"

Opposite the entrance to the Sevres Museum in the old town of Sevres, in France, stands a handsome bronze statue of Bernard Palissy, the potter. Within the museum are some exquisite pieces of pottery known as "Palissy ware." They are specimens of the art of Palissy, who spent the best years of his life toiling to discover the mode of making white enamel.

The story of his trials and sufferings in seeking to learn the secret, and of his final triumph over all difficulties, is an inspiring one.

Born in the south of France, as far back as the year 1509, Bernard Palissy did not differ much from an intelligent, high-spirited American boy of the twentieth century. His parents were poor, and he had few of the advantages within the reach of the humblest child in the United States to-day. In spite of poverty, he was cheerful, light hearted, and happy in his great love for nature, which distinguished him all through life. The forest was his playground, his companions the birds, insects, and other living things that made their home there.

From the first, Nature was his chief teacher. It was from her, and her alone, he learned the lessons that in after years made him famous both as a potter and a scientist. The habit of observation seemed natural to him, for without suggestions from books or older heads, his eyes and ears noticed all that the nature student of our day is drilled into observing.

The free, outdoor life of the forest helped to give the boy the strength of mind and body which afterward enabled him, in spite of the most discouraging conditions, to pursue his ideal. He was taught how to read and write, and from his father learned how to paint on glass. From him he also learned the names and some of the properties of the minerals employed in painting glass. All the knowledge that in after years made him an artist, a scientist, and a writer, was the result of his unaided study of nature. To books he was indebted for only the smallest part of what he knew.

Happy and hopeful, sunshiny of face and disposition, Bernard grew from childhood to youth. Then, when he was about eighteen, there came into his heart a longing to try his fortune in the great world which lay beyond his forest home. Like most country-bred boys of his age, he felt that he had grown too large for the parent nest and must try his wings elsewhere. In his case there was, indeed, little to induce an ambitious boy to stay at home. The trade of glass painting, which in previous years had been a profitable one, had at that time fallen somewhat out of favor, and there was not enough work to keep father and son busy.

When he shouldered his scanty wallet and bade farewell to father and mother, and the few friends and neighbors he knew in the straggling forest hamlet, Bernard Palissy closed the first chapter of his life. The second was a long period of travel and self-education.

He wandered through the forest of Ardennes, making observations and collecting specimens of minerals, plants, reptiles, and insects. He spent some years in the upper Pyrenees, at Tarbes. From Antwerp in the east he bent his steps to Brest, in the most westerly part of Brittany, and from Montpellier to Nismes he traveled across France. During his wanderings he supported himself by painting on glass, portrait painting (which he practiced after a fashion), surveying, and planning sites for houses and gardens. In copying or inventing patterns for painted windows, he had acquired a knowledge of geometry and considerable skill in the use of a rule and compass. His love of knowledge for its own sake made him follow up the study of geometry, as far as he could pursue it, and hence his skill as a surveyor.

At this time young Palissy had no other object in life than to learn. His eager, inquiring mind was ever on the alert. Wherever his travels led him, he sought information of men and nature, always finding the latter his chief instructor. He painted and planned that he might live to probe her secrets. But the time was fast approaching when a new interest should come into his life and overshadow all others.

After ten or twelve years of travel, he married and settled in Saintes where he pursued, as his services were required, the work of glass painter and surveyor. Before long he grew dissatisfied with the dull routine of his daily life. He felt that he ought to do more than make a living for his wife and children. There were two babies now to be cared for as well as his wife, and he could not shoulder his wallet, as in the careless days of his boyhood, and wander away in search of knowledge or fortune.

About this time an event happened which changed his whole life. He was shown a beautiful cup of Italian manufacture. I give in his own words a description of the cup, and the effect the sight of it had on him. "An earthen cup," he says, "turned and enameled with so much beauty, that from that time I entered into controversy with my own thoughts, recalling to mind several suggestions that some people had made to me in fun, when I was painting portraits. Then, seeing that these were falling out of request in the country where I dwelt, and that glass painting was also little patronized, I began to think that if I should discover how to make enamels, I could make earthen vessels and other things very prettily, because God has gifted me with some knowledge of drawing."

His ambition was fired at once. A definite purpose formed itself in his mind. He knew nothing whatever of pottery. No man in France knew the secret of enameling, which made the Italian cup so beautiful, and Palissy had not the means to go to Italy, where he probably could have learned it. He resolved to study the nature and properties of clays, and not to rest until he had discovered the secret of the white enamel. Delightful visions filled his imagination. He thought within himself that he would become the prince of potters, and would provide his wife and children with all the luxuries that money could buy. "Thereafter," he wrote, "regardless of the fact that I had no knowledge of clays, I began to seek for the enamels as a man gropes in the dark."

Palissy was a young man when he began his search for the enamel; he was past middle life when his labors were finally rewarded. Groping like a man in the dark, as he himself said, he experimented for years with clays and chemicals, but with small success. He built with his own hands a furnace at the back of his little cottage in which to carry on his experiments. At first his enthusiasm inspired his wife and neighbors with the belief that he would succeed in his efforts. But time went on, and as one experiment after another failed or was only partially successful, one and all lost faith in him. He had no friend or helper to buoy him up under his many disappointments. Even his wife reproached him for neglecting his regular work and reducing herself and her children to poverty and want, while he wasted his time and strength in chasing a dream. His neighbors jeered at him as a madman, one who put his plain duty aside for the gratification of what seemed to their dull minds merely a whim. His poor wife could hardly be blamed for reproaching him. She could neither understand nor sympathize with his hopes and fears, while she knew that if he followed his trade, he could at least save his family from want. It was a trying time for both of them. But who ever heard tell of an artist, inventor, discoverer, or genius of any kind being deterred by poverty, abuse, ridicule, or obstacles of any kind from the pursuit of an ideal!

After many painful efforts, the poor glass painter had succeeded in producing a substance which he believed to be white enamel. He spread it on a number of earthenware pots which he had made, and placed them in his furnace. The extremities to which he was reduced to supply heat to the furnace are set forth in his own words: "Having," he says, "covered the new pieces with the said enamel, I put them into the furnace, still keeping the fire at its height; but thereupon occurred to me a new misfortune which caused great mortification, namely, that the wood having failed me, I was forced to burn the palings which maintained the boundaries of my garden; which being burnt also, I was forced to burn the tables and the flooring of my house, to cause the melting of the second composition. I suffered an anguish that I cannot speak, for I was quite exhausted and dried up by the heat of the furnace. Further, to console me, I was the object of mockery; and even those from whom solace was due ran crying through the town that I was burning my floors, and in this way my credit was taken from me, and I was regarded as a madman.

"Others said that I was laboring to make false money, which was a scandal under which I pined away, and slipped with bowed head through the streets like a man put to shame. No one gave me consolation, but, on the contrary, men jested at me, saying, 'It was right for him to die of hunger, seeing that he had left off following his trade!' All these things assailed my ears when I passed through the street; but for all that, there still remained some hope which encouraged and sustained me, inasmuch as the last trials had turned out tolerably well; and thereafter I thought that I knew enough to get my own living, although I was far enough from that (as you shall hear afterward)."

This latest experiment filled him with joy, for he had at last discovered the secret of the enamel. But there was yet much to be learned, and several years more of extreme poverty and suffering had to be endured before his labors were rewarded with complete success. But it came at last in overflowing measure, as it almost invariably does to those who are willing to work and suffer privation and persevere to the end.

His work as a potter brought Palissy fame and riches. At the invitation of Catherine de' Medici, wife of King Henry II of France, he removed to Paris. He established a workshop in the vicinity of the royal Palace of the Tuileries, and was thereafter known as "Bernard of the Tuileries." He was employed by the king and queen and some of the greatest nobles of France to embellish their palaces and gardens with the products of his beautiful art.

Notwithstanding his lack of schooling, Bernard Palissy was one of the most learned men of his day. He founded a Museum of Natural History, wrote valuable books on natural science, and for several years delivered lectures on the same subject. His lectures were attended by the most advanced scholars of Paris, who were astonished at the extent and accuracy of his knowledge of nature. But he was as modest as he was wise and good, and when people wondered at his learning, he would reply with the most unaffected simplicity, "I have had no other book than the sky and the earth, known to all."

No more touching story of success, in spite of great difficulties, than Bernard Palissy's has been written. It is bad to think that after the terrible trials which he endured for the sake of his art, his last years also should have been clouded by misfortune. During the civil war which raged in France between the Huguenots and the Catholics, he was, on account of his religious views, imprisoned in the Bastile, where he died in 1589, at the age of eighty.

***

HOW THE "LEARNED BLACKSMITH" FOUND TIME

"The loss of an hour," says the philosopher, Leibnitz, "is the loss of a part of life." This is a truth that has been appreciated by most men who have risen to distinction,—who have been world benefactors. The lives of those great moral heroes put to shame the laggard youth of to-day, who so often grumbles: "I have no time. If I didn't have to work all day, I could accomplish something. I could read and educate myself. But if a fellow has to grub away ten or twelve hours out of the twenty-four, what time is left to do anything for one's self?"

How much spare time had Elihu Burritt, "the youngest of many brethren," as he himself quaintly puts it, born in a humble home in New Britain, Connecticut, reared amid toil and poverty? Yet, during his father's long illness, and after his death, when Elihu was but a lad in his teens, with the family partially dependent upon the work of his hands, he found time,—if only a few moments,—at the end of a fourteen-hour day of labor, for his books.

While working at his trade as a blacksmith, he solved problems in arithmetic and algebra while his irons were heating. Over the forge also appeared a Latin grammar and a Greek lexicon; and, while with sturdy blows the ambitious youth of sixteen shaped the iron on the anvil, he fixed in his mind conjugations and declensions.

How did this man, born nearly a century ago, possessing none of the advantages within reach of the poorest and humblest boy of to-day, become one of the brightest ornaments in the world of letters, a leader in the reform movements of his generation?

Apparently no more talented than his nine brothers and sisters, by improving every opportunity he could wring from a youth of unremitting toil, his love for knowledge grew with what it fed upon, and carried him to undreamed-of heights. In palaces and council halls, the words of the "Learned Blacksmith" were listened to with the closest attention and deference.

Read the life of Elihu Burritt, and you will be ashamed to grumble that you have no time—no chance for self-improvement.

***

THE LEGEND OF WILLIAM TELL

"Ye crags and peaks, I'm with you once again! I hold to you the hands you first beheld, to show they still are free. Methinks I hear a spirit in your echoes answer me, and bid your tenant welcome to his home again! O sacred forms, how proud you look! how high you lift your heads into the sky! how huge you are, how mighty, and how free! Ye are the things that tower, that shine; whose smile makes glad—whose frown is terrible; whose forms, robed or unrobed, do all the impress wear of awe divine. Ye guards of liberty, I'm with you once again! I call to you with all my voice! I hold my hands to you to show they still are free. I rush to you as though I could embrace you!"

What schoolboy or schoolgirl is not familiar with those stirring lines from "William Tell's Address to His Native Mountains," by J. M. Knowles? And the story of William Tell,—is it not dear to every heart that loves liberty? Though modern history declares it to be purely mythical, its popularity remains unaffected. It will live forever in the traditions of Switzerland, dear to the hearts of her people as their native mountains, and even more full of interest to the stranger than authentic history.

"His image [Tell's]," says Lamartine, "with those of his wife and children, are inseparably connected with the majestic, rural, and smiling landscapes of Helvetia, the modern Arcadia of Europe. As often as the traveler visits these peculiar regions; as often as the unconquered summits of Mont Blanc, St. Gothard, and the Rigi, present themselves to his eyes in the vast firmament as the ever-enduring symbols of liberty; whenever the lake of the Four Cantons presents a vessel wavering on the blue surface of its waters; whenever the cascade bursts in thunder from the heights of the Splugen, and shivers itself upon the rocks like tyranny against free hearts; whenever the ruins of an Austrian fortress darken with the remains of frowning walls the round eminences of Uri or Claris; and whenever a calm sunbeam gilds on the declivity of a village the green velvet of the meadows where the herds are feeding to the tinkling of bells and the echo of the Ranz des Vaches—so often the imagination traces in all these varied scenes the hat on the summit of the pole—the archer condemned to aim at the apple placed on the head of his own child—the mark hurled to the ground, transfixed by the unerring arrow—the father chained to the bottom of the boat, subduing night, the storm, and his own indignation, to save his executioner—and finally, the outraged husband, threatened with the loss of all he holds most dear, yielding to the impulse of nature, and in his turn striking the murderer with a deathblow."

The story which tradition hands down as the origin of the freedom of Switzerland dates back to the beginning of the fourteenth century. At that time Switzerland was under the sovereignty of the emperor of Germany, who ruled over Central Europe. Count Rudolph of Hapsburg, a Swiss by birth, who had been elected to the imperial throne in 1273, made some efforts to save his countrymen from the oppression of a foreign yoke. His son, Albert, Archduke of Austria, who succeeded him in 1298, inherited none of his sympathies for Switzerland. On his accession to the throne Albert resolved to curtail the liberties still enjoyed by the inhabitants of some of the cantons, and to bend the whole of the Swiss people to his will.

The mountaineers of the cantons of Schwytz, Uri, and Unterwalden recognized no authority but that of the emperor; while the peasants of the neighboring valleys were at the mercy of local tyrants—the great nobles and their allies.

In order to carry out his project of subjecting all to the same yoke, Albert of Austria appointed governors to rule over the semi-free provinces or cantons. These governors, who bore the official title of Bailiffs of the Emperor, exercised absolute authority over the people. Men, women, and children were at their mercy, and were treated as mere chattels—the property of their rulers. Insult and outrage were heaped upon them until their lives became almost unendurable.

An instance of the manner in which these petty tyrants used their authority is related of the bailiff Landenberg, who ruled over Unterwalden.

For some trumped-up offense of which a young peasant, named Arnold of Melcthal, was accused, his oxen were confiscated by Landenberg. The deputy sent to seize the animals, which Landenberg really coveted for his own, said sneeringly to Arnold, "If peasants wish for bread, they must draw the plow themselves." Roused to fury by this taunt, Arnold attempted to resist the seizure of his property, and in so doing broke an arm of one of the deputy's men. He then fled to the mountains; but he could not hide himself from the vengeance of Landenberg. The peasant's aged father was arrested by order of the bailiff, and his eyes put out in punishment for his son's offense. "That puncture," says an old chronicler, "went so deep into many a heart that numbers resolved to die rather than leave it unrequited."

But the crudest and most vindictive of the Austrian or German bailiffs, as they were interchangeably called, was one Hermann Gessler. He had built himself a fortress, which he called "Uri's Restraint," and there he felt secure from all attacks.

This man was the terror of the whole district. His name was a synonym for all that was base, brutal, and tyrannical. Neither the property, the lives, nor the honor of the people were respected by him. His hatred and contempt for the peasants were so great that the least semblance of prosperity among them aroused his ire.

One day while riding with an armed escort through the canton of Schwytz, he noticed a comfortable-looking dwelling which was being built by one Werner Stauffacher. Turning to his followers, he cried, "Is it not shameful that miserable serfs like these should be permitted to build such houses when huts would be too good for them?" "Let this be finished," said his chief attendant; "we shall then sculpture over the gate the arms of the emperor, and a little time will show whether the builder has the audacity to dispute possession with us." The answer pleased Gessler, who replied, "Thou art right," and, planning future vengeance, he passed on with his escort.

The wife of Stauffacher, who had been standing near the new building, but concealed from Gessler and his men, heard the conversation, and reported it to her husband. The latter, filled with indignation, without uttering a word, arose and started for the home of his father-in-law, Walter Furst, in the village of Attinghaussen.

On his arrival Staffaucher was cordially welcomed by his father-in-law, who placed refreshments before him, and waited for him to explain the object of his visit. Pushing aside the food, he said, "I have made a vow never again to taste wine or swallow meat until we cease to be slaves." Stauffacher then related what had happened. Furst's anger was kindled by the recital. Both men were roused to such a pitch that they resolved, then and there, to free themselves and their countrymen from the chains which bound them, or die in the attempt. They conversed far into the night, making plans for the gaining of national independence. Then they sought out in his hiding-place Arnold of Melchthal, the young peasant whom Landenberg had so cruelly persecuted. In him they found, as they expected, an ardent supporter of their plans.

The three conspirators, Stauffacher, Furst, and Melchthal, represented different cantons; one belonging to Schwytz, another to Uri, and the third to Unterwalden. They hoped to form a league and unite the three cantons against the power of Austria. In pursuance of their plans, each pledged himself to select from among the most persecuted and the most daring in their respective cantons ten others to join them in the cause of liberty.

On the night of November 7, or 17 (the date is variously given), in the year 1307, the confederates met together in a secluded mountain spot called Rutli. There they bound themselves by an oath, the terms of which embodied their purpose: "We swear in the presence of God, before whom kings and people are equal, to live or die for our fellow-countrymen; to undertake and sustain all in common; neither to suffer injustice nor to commit injury; to respect the rights and property of the Count of Hapsburg; to do no violence to the imperial bailiffs, but to put an end to their tyranny." They fixed upon January 1, 1308, as the day for a general uprising.

Events were gradually shaping themselves for the appearance of William Tell on the scene. Up to this time his name does not appear in the annals of his country. The bold peasant of Uri was so little prominent among his countrymen that, according to some versions of the legend, although a son-in-law of Walter Furst, he had not been chosen among the thirty conspirators summoned to the meeting at Rutli. This, however, is contradicted by another, which asserts that he was "one of the oath-bound men of Rutli."

The various divergences in the different versions of the legend do not affect its main features, on which all the chroniclers are agreed. It was the crowning insult to his country which indisputably brought Tell into prominence and made his name forever famous.

Gessler's hatred of the people daily increased, and was constantly showing itself in every form of petty tyranny that a mean and wicked nature could devise. He noticed the growing discontent among the peasantry, but instead of trying to allay it, he determined to humiliate them still more. For this purpose he had a pole, surmounted by the ducal cap of Austria, erected in the market square of the village of Altdorf, and issued a command that all who passed it should bow before the symbol of imperial rule. Guards were placed by the pole with orders to make prisoners of all who refused to pay homage to the ducal cap.

William Tell, a bold hunter and skillful boatman of Uri, passing by one day, with his little son, Walter, refused to bend his knee before the symbol of foreign oppression. He was seized at once by the guards and carried before the bailiff.

There is considerable contradiction at this point as to whether Tell was at once carried before the bailiff or bound to the pole, where he remained, guarded by the soldiers, until the bailiff, returning the same day from a hunting expedition, appeared upon the scene. Schiller, in his drama of "William Tell," adopts the latter version of the story.

According to the drama, Tell is represented as being bound to the pole. In a short time he is surrounded by friends and neighbors. Among them are his father-in-law, Walter Furst, Werner Stauffacher, and Arnold of Melchthal. They advance to rescue the prisoner. The guards cry in a loud voice: "Revolt! Rebellion! Treason! Sedition! Help! Protect the agents of the law!"

Gessler and his party hear the cries, and rush to the support of the guards. Gessler cries in a loud authoritative voice: "Wherefore is this assembly of people? Who called for help? What does all this mean? I demand to know the cause of this!"

Then, addressing himself particularly to one of the guards and pointing to Tell, he says: "Stand forward! Who art thou, and why dost thou hold that man a prisoner?"

"Most mighty lord," replies the guard, "I am one of your soldiers placed here as a sentinel over that hat. I seized this man in the act of disobedience, for refusing to salute it. I was about to carry him to prison in compliance with your orders, and the populace were preparing to rescue him by force."

After questioning Tell, whose answers are not satisfactory, the bailiff pronounces sentence upon him. The sentence is that he shall shoot at an apple placed on the head of his little son, Walter, and if he fails to hit the mark he shall die.

"My lord," cries the agonized parent; "what horrible command is this you lay upon me? What! aim at a mark placed on the head of my dear child? No, no, it is impossible that such a thought could enter your imagination. In the name of the God of mercy, you cannot seriously impose that trial on a father."

"Thou shalt aim at an apple placed on the head of thy son. I will and I command it," repeats the tyrant.

"I! William Tell! aim with my own crossbow at the head of my own offspring! I would rather die a thousand deaths."

"Thou shall shoot, or assuredly thou diest with thy son!"

"Become the murderer of my child! My lord, you have no son—you cannot have the feelings of a father's heart!"

Gessler's friends interfere in behalf of the unhappy father, and plead for mercy. But all appeal is in vain. The tyrant is determined on carrying out his sentence.

The father and son are placed at a distance of eighty paces apart. An apple is placed on the boy's head, and the father is commanded to hit the mark. He hesitates and trembles.

"Why dost thou hesitate?" questions his persecutor. "Thou hast deserved death, and I could compel thee to undergo the punishment; but in my clemency I place thy fate in thy own skillful hands. He who is the master of his destiny cannot complain that his sentence is a severe one. Thou art proud of thy steady eye and unerring aim; now, hunter, is the moment to prove thy skill. The object is worthy of thee—the prize is worth contending for. To strike the center of a target is an ordinary achievement; but the true master of his art is he who is always certain, and whose heart, hand, and eye are firm and steady under every trial."

At length Tell nerves himself for the ordeal, raises his bow, and takes aim at the target on his son's head. Before firing, however, he concealed a second arrow under his vest. His movement did not escape Gessler's notice.

The marksman fires. The apple falls from his boy's head, cleft in twain by the arrow.

Even Gessler is loud in his admiration of Tell's skill. "By heaven," he cries, "he has clove the apple exactly in the center. Let us do justice; it is indeed a masterpiece of skill."

Tell's friends congratulate him. He is about to set out for his home with the child who has been saved to him from the very jaws of death as it were. But Gessler stays him.

"Thou hast concealed a second arrow in thy bosom," he says, sternly addressing Tell. "What didst thou intend to do with it?" Tell replies that such is the custom of all hunters.

Gessler is not satisfied and urges him to confess his real motive. "Speak truly and frankly," he says; "say what thou wilt, I promise thee thy life. To what purpose didst thou destine the second arrow?"

Tell can no longer restrain his indignation, and, fixing his eyes steadily on Gessler, he answers "Well then, my lord, since you assure my life, I will speak the truth without reserve. If I had struck my beloved child, with the second arrow I would have transpierced thy heart. Assuredly that time I should not have missed my mark."

"Villain!" exclaims Gessler, "I have promised thee life upon my knightly word; I will keep my pledge. But since I know thee now, and thy rebellious heart, I will remove thee to a place where thou shalt never more behold the light of sun or moon. Thus only shall I be sheltered from thy arrows."

He orders the guards to seize and bind Tell, saying, "I will myself at once conduct him to Kussnacht."

The fortress of Kussnacht was situated on the summit of Mount Rigi between Lake Lucerne, or the Lake of the Four Cantons as it is sometimes called, and Lake Zug. It was reached by crossing Lake Lucerne.

The prisoner was placed bound in the bottom of a boat, and with his guards, the rowers, an inexperienced pilot, and Gessler in command, the boat was headed for Kussnacht.

When about halfway across the lake a sudden and violent storm overwhelmed the party. They were in peril of their lives. The rowers and pilot were panic-stricken, and powerless in face of the danger that threatened them.

Tell's fame as a boatman was as widespread as that of his skill as an archer. The rowers cried aloud in their terror that he was the only man in Switzerland that could save them from death. Gessler immediately commanded him to be released from his bonds and given the helm.

Tell succeeded in guiding the vessel to the shore. Then seizing his bow and arrows, which his captors had thrown beside him, he sprang ashore at a point known as "Tell's Leap." The boat, rebounding, after he leaped from it was again driven out on the lake before any of the remainder of its occupants could effect a landing. After a time, however, the fury of the storm abated, and they reached the shore in safety.

In the meantime Tell had concealed himself in a defile in the mountain through which Gessler would have to pass on his way to Kussnacht. There he lay in wait for his persecutor who followed in hot pursuit.

Vowing vengeance as he went, Gessler declared that if the fugitive did not give himself up to justice, every day that passed by should cost him the life of his wife or one of his children. While the tyrant was yet speaking, an arrow shot by an unerring hand pierced his heart. Tell had taken vengeance into his own hands.

The death of Gessler was the signal for a general uprising. The oath-bound men of Rutli saw that this was their great opportunity. They called to their countrymen to follow them to freedom or death.

Gessler's crowning act of tyranny—his inhuman punishment of Tell—had roused the spirit of rebellion in the hearts of even the meekest and most submissive of the peasants. Gladly, then, did they respond to the call of the leaders of the insurrection.

The legend says that on New Year's Eve, 1308, Stauffacher, with a chosen band of followers, climbed the mountain which led to Landenberg's fortress castle of Rotzberg. There they were assisted by an inmate of the castle, a young girl whose lover was among the rebels. She threw a rope out of one of the windows of the castle, and by it her countrymen climbed one after another into the castle. They seized the bailiff, Landenberg, and confined him in one of the dungeons of his own castle. Next day the conspirators were reinforced by another party who gained entrance to the castle by means of a clever ruse. Landenberg and his men were given their freedom by the peasants on condition that they would quit Switzerland forever.

The castle of Uri was attacked and taken possession of by Walter Furst and William Tell, while other strongholds were captured by Arnold of Melchthal and his associates.

Bonfires blazed all over the country. The dawn of Switzerland's freedom had appeared. The reign of tyranny was doomed. William Tell was the hero of the hour, and ever since his name has been enshrined in the hearts of his countrymen as the watchword of their liberties. Even to this day, as history tells us, the Swiss peasant cherishes the belief that "Tell and the three men of Rutli are asleep in the mountains, but will awake to the rescue of their land should tyranny ever again enchain it."

Lamartine, to whose story of William Tell the writer is indebted, commenting on the legend says: "The artlessness of this history resembles a poem; it is a pastoral song in which a single drop of blood is mingled with the dew upon a leaf or a tuft of grass. Providence seems thus to delight in providing for every free community, as the founder of their independence, a fabulous or actual hero, conformable to the local situation, manners, and character of each particular race. To a rustic, pastoral people, like the Swiss, is given for their liberator a noble peasant; to a proud, aspiring race, such as the Americans, an honest soldier. Two distinct symbols, standing erect by the cradles of the two modern liberties of the world to personify their opposite natures: on the one hand Tell, with his arrow and the apple; on the other, Washington, with his sword and the law."

***

"WESTWARD HO!"

When the current serves, the unseen monitor that directs our affairs bids us step aboard our craft, and, with hand firmly grasping the helm, steer boldly for the distant goal.

Philip D. Armour, the open-handed, large-hearted merchant prince, who has left a standing memorial to his benevolence in the Armour Institute at Chicago, heard the call to put to sea when in his teens.

It came during the gold fever, which raged with such intensity from 1849 to 1851, when the wildest stories were afloat of the treasures that were daily being dug out of the earth in California. The brain of the sturdy youth, whose Scotch and Puritan blood tingled for some broader field than the village store and his father's farm in Stockbridge, New York, was haunted by the tales of adventure and fortune wafted across the continent from the new El Dorado. "I brooded over the difference," he says, "between tossing hay in the hot sun and digging gold by handfuls, until, one day, I threw down the pitchfork, went to the house, and told mother that I had quit that kind of work."

Armour was nineteen years old when he determined to seek his fortune in California. His determination once formed, he lost no time in carrying it out. As much of the journey across the plains was to be made on foot, he first provided himself with a pair of stout boots. Then he packed his extra clothing in an old carpetbag, and with a light heart bade his family good-by.

He had induced a young friend, Calvin Gilbert, to accompany him in his search for fortune. The two youths joined the motley crowd of adventurers who were flocking from all quarters to the Land of Promise, and set out on their journey.

Tramping over the plains, crossing rivers in tow-boats and ferryboats, and riding in trains and on wagons when they could, the adventurers, after many weary months, reached their destination. During the journey young Armour became sick, but was tenderly nursed back to health by his companion.

"I had scarcely any money when I arrived at the gold fields," said Armour, "but I struck right out and found a place where I could dig, and in a little time I struck pay dirt."

He entered into partnership with a Mr. Croarkin, and, with characteristic energy, kept digging and taking his turn at the rude housekeeping in the shanty which he and his partner shared. "Croarkin would cook one week," he says, "and I the next, and we would have a clean-up Sunday morning We baked our own bread, and kept a few hens, too, which supplied us with fresh eggs."

The young gold hunter, however, did not find nuggets as "plentiful as blackberries," but he found within himself that which led him to a bonanza far exceeding his wildest dreams of "finds" in the gold fields.

He discovered his business ability; he learned how to economize, how to rely upon himself, even to the extent of baking his own bread.

***

THREE GREAT AMERICAN SONGS AND THEIR AUTHORS

I. THE STAR-SPANGLED BANNER

"Poetry and music," says Sir John Lubbock, "unite in song. From the earliest ages song has been the sweet companion of labor. The rude chant of the boatman floats upon the water, the shepherd sings upon the hill, the milkmaid in the dairy, the plowman in the field. Every trade, every occupation, every act and scene of life, has long had its own especial music. The bride went to her marriage, the laborer to his work, the old man to his last long rest, each with appropriate and immemorial music."

It is strange that Lubbock did not mention specifically the power of music in inspiring the soldier as he marches to the defense of his country, or in arousing the spirit of patriotism and kindling the love of country, whether in peace or war, in every bosom. "Let me make the songs of a country," Fletcher of Saltoun has well said, "and I care not who makes its laws."

Not to know the words and the air of the national anthem or chief patriotic songs of one's country is considered little less than a disgrace. To know something of their authors and the occasion which inspired them, or the conditions under which they were composed, gives additional interest to the songs themselves.

Francis Scott Key, author of "The Star-spangled Banner," one of the, if not the most, popular of our national songs, was born in Frederick County, Maryland, on August 1, 1779. He was the son of John Ross Key, an officer in the Revolutionary army.

Young Key's early education was carried on under the direction of his father. Later he became a student in St. John's College, from which institution he was graduated in his nineteenth year. Immediately after his graduation he began to study law under his uncle, Philip Barton Key, one of the ablest lawyers of his time. He was admitted to the bar in 1801, and commenced to practice in Fredericktown, Maryland, where he won the reputation of an eloquent advocate. After a few years' practice in Fredericktown, he removed to Washington, where he was appointed district attorney for the District of Columbia.

Young Key was as widely known and admired as a writer of hymns and ballads as he was as a lawyer of promise. But the production of the popular national anthem which crowned him with immortality has so overshadowed the rest of his life work that we remember him only as its author.

The occasion which inspired "The Star-spangled Banner" must always be memorable in the annals of our country. The war with the British had been about two years in progress, when, in August, 1814, a British fleet arrived in the Chesapeake, and an army under General Ross landed about forty miles from the city of Washington.

The army took possession of Washington, burnt the capitol, the President's residence, and other public buildings, and then sailed around by the sea to attack Baltimore. The fleet was to bombard Fort McHenry, while the land forces were to attack the city.

The commanding officers of the fleet and land army, Admiral Cockburn and General Ross, made their headquarters in Upper Marlboro, Maryland, at the house of Dr. William Beanes, whom they held as their prisoner.

Francis Scott Key, who was a warm friend of Dr. Beanes, went to President Madison in order to enlist his aid in securing the release of Beanes. The president furnished Key with a vessel, and instructed John L. Skinner, agent for the exchange of prisoners, to accompany him under a flag of truce to the British fleet.

The British commander agreed to release Dr. Beanes, but would not permit Key and his party to return then, lest they should carry back important information to the American side. He boastingly declared, however, that the defense could hold out only a few hours, and that Baltimore would then be in the hands of the British.

Skinner and Key were sent on board the Surprise, which was under the command of Admiral Cockburn's son. But after a short time they were allowed to return to their own vessel, and from its deck they saw the American flag waving over Fort McHenry and witnessed the bombardment.

All through the night the furious attack of the British continued. The roar of cannon and the bursting of shells was incessant. It is said that as many as fifteen hundred shells were hurled at the fort.

Shortly before daybreak the firing ceased. Key and his companions waited in painful suspense to know the result. In the intense silence that followed the cannonading, each one asked himself if the flag of his country was still waving on high, or if it had been hauled down to give place to that of England. They strained their eyes in the direction of Baltimore, but the darkness revealed nothing.

At last day dawned, and to their delight the little party saw the American flag still floating over Fort McHenry. Key's heart was stirred to its depths, and in a glow of patriotic enthusiasm he immediately wrote down a rough draft of "The Star-spangled Banner."

On his arrival in Baltimore he perfected the first copy of the song, and gave it to Captain Benjamin Eades, of the 27th Baltimore Regiment, saying that he wished it to be sung to the air of "Anacreon in Heaven." Eades had it put in type, and took the first proof to a famous old tavern near the Holliday Street Theater, a favorite resort of actors and literary people of that day. The verses were read to the company assembled there, and Frederick Durang, an actor, was asked to sing them to the air designated by the author. Durang, mounting a chair, sang as requested. The song was enthusiastically received. From that moment it became the great popular favorite that it has ever since been, and that it will continue to be as long as the American republic exists.

Key died in Baltimore on January 11, 1843. A monument was erected to his memory by the munificence of James Lick, a Californian millionaire. The sculptor to whom the work was intrusted was the celebrated W. W. Story, who completed it in 1887. The monument, which is fifty-one feet high, stands in Golden Gate Park, San Francisco. It is built of travertine, in the form of a double arch, under which a bronze statue of Key is seated. A bronze figure, representing America with an unfolded flag, supports the arch.

On the occasion of the unveiling of this statue, the New York Home Journal contained an appreciative criticism of Key as a poet, and the following estimate of his greatest production.

"The poetry of the 'Star-spangled Banner' has touches of delicacy for which one looks in vain in most national odes, and is as near a true poem as any national ode ever was. The picture of the 'dawn's early light' and the tricolor, half concealed, half disclosed, amid the mists that wreathed the battle-sounding Patapsco, is a true poetic concept.

"The 'Star-spangled Banner' has the peculiar merit of not being a tocsin song, like the 'Marseillaise.' Indeed, there is not a restful, soothing, or even humane sentiment in all that stormy shout. It is the scream of oppressed humanity against its oppressor, presaging a more than quid pro quo; and it fitly prefigured the sight of that long file of tumbrils bearing to the Place de la Revolution the fairest scions of French aristocracy. On the other hand, 'God Save the King,' in its original, has one or two lines as grotesque as 'Yankee Doodle' itself; yet we have paraphrased it in 'America,' and made it a hymn meet for all our churches. But the 'Star-spangled Banner' combines dignity and beauty, and it would be hard to find a line of it that could be improved upon."

Over the simple grave of Francis Scott Key, in Frederick, Maryland, there is no other monument than the "star-spangled banner." In storm and in sunshine, in summer and in winter, its folds ever float over the resting place of the man who has immortalized it in verse. No other memorial could so fitly commemorate the life and death of this simple, dignified, patriotic American.

"A sweet, noble life," says a recent writer, "was that of the author of our favorite national hymn—a life of ideal refinement, piety, scholarly gentleness. Little did he think that his voice would be the storm song, the victor shout, of conquering America to resound down and down the ages!"

THE STAR-SPANGLED BANNER

Oh! say, can you see, by the dawn's early light,
    What so proudly we hailed at the twilight's last gleaming?
Whose broad stripes and bright stars through the perilous fight,
    O'er the rampart we watched, were so gallantly streaming,
And the rocket's red glare, the bombs bursting in air,
Gave proof through the night that our flag was still there,
    Oh! say, does that star-spangled banner yet wave
    O'er the land of the free and the home of the brave?

On the shore, dimly seen through the mists of the deep,
    Where the foe's haughty host in dread silence reposes,
What is that which the breeze, o'er the towering steep,
    As it fitfully blows, half conceals, half discloses?
Now it catches the gleam of the morning's first beam,
In full glory reflected now shines on the stream,
    'Tis the star-spangled banner' oh, long may it wave
    O'er the land of the free and the home of the brave!

And where is that band, who so vauntingly swore
    That the havoc of war and the battle's confusion
A home and a country should leave us no more?
    Their blood has washed out their foul footsteps' pollution.
No refuge could save the hireling and slave,
From the terror of death and the gloom of the grave,
    And the star spangled banner in triumph shall wave
    O'er the land of the free and the home of the brave!

Oh! thus be it ever, when freemen shall stand
    Between their loved homes and the war's desolation,
Blest with victory and peace, may the heaven rescued land
    Praise the power that has made and preserved us a nation.

Then conquer we must, for our cause it is just,
And this be our motto, "In God is our trust"
    And the star-spangled banner in triumph shall wave
    O'er the land of the free and the home of the brave!

II. AMERICA

"And there's a nice youngster of excellent pith;
Fate tried to conceal him by naming him Smith!
But he shouted a song for the brave and the free—
Just read on his medal, 'My Country of Thee.'"

In these lines of his famous Reunion Poem, "The Boys," Dr. Oliver Wendell Holmes commemorated his old friend and college-mate, Dr. Samuel Francis Smith, author of "America."

Samuel Francis Smith was born in Boston, Massachusetts, on October 21, 1808. He attended the Latin School in his native city, and it is said that when only twelve years old he could "talk Latin." He entered Harvard College, Cambridge, Massachusetts, in 1825, and graduated in the famous class of 1829, of which Dr. Oliver Wendell Holmes, James Freeman Clarke, William E. Channing, and other celebrated Americans were members.

Dr. Smith, like so many other noted men, "worked his way through college." He did this principally by coaching other students, and by making translations from the German "Conversations-Lexicon" for the "American Cyclopedia."

After graduating from Harvard, he immediately entered Andover Theological Seminary. Three years later, in 1832, he wrote, among others, his most famous hymn, "America," of which the "National Cyclopedia of American Biography" says, "It has found its way wherever an American heart beats or the English language is spoken, and has probably proved useful in stirring the patriotic spirit of the American people."

Dr. Smith himself often said that he had heard "America" sung "halfway round the world, under the earth in the caverns of Manitou, Colorado, and almost above the earth near the top of Pike's Peak."

The hymn, as every child knows, is sung to the air of the national anthem of England,—"God Save the King." The author came upon it in a book of German music, and by it was inspired to write the words of "America," a work which he accomplished in half an hour. Many years after, referring to its impromptu composition, he wrote: "If I had anticipated the future of it, doubtless I should have taken more pains with it. Such as it is, I am glad to have contributed this mite to the cause of American freedom."

In a magazine article, written several years ago, Mr. Herbert Heywood gave an interesting account of an interview with Dr. Smith, who told him the story of the writing of the hymn himself.

"'I wrote "America,"' he said, 'when I was a theological student at Andover, during my last year there. In February, 1832, I was poring over a German book of patriotic songs which Lowell Mason, of Boston, had sent me to translate, when I came upon one with a tune of great majesty. I hummed it over, and was struck with the ease with which the accompanying German words fell into the music. I saw it was a patriotic song, and while I was thinking of translating it, I felt an impulse to write an American patriotic hymn. I reached my hand for a bit of waste paper, and, taking my quill pen, wrote the four verses in half an hour. I sent it with some translations of the German songs to Lowell Mason, and the next thing I knew of it I was told it had been sung by the Sunday-school children at Park Street Church, Boston, at the following Fourth of July celebration. The house where I was living at the time was on the Andover turnpike, a little north of the seminary building. I have been in the house since I left it in September, 1832, but never went into my old room.'" This room is now visited by patriotic Americans from every part of the country.

Two years after "America" was written, Dr. Smith became pastor of the First Baptist Church in Waterville, Maine, and also professor of modern languages in Waterville College, which is now known as Colby University. His great industry and zeal, both as a clergyman and student and teacher of languages, enabled him to perform the duties of both positions successfully. He was a noted linguist, and could read books in fifteen different languages. He could converse in most of the modern European tongues, and at eighty-six was engaged in studying Russian.

In 1842 Dr. Smith was made pastor of the First Baptist Church, Newton Center, Massachusetts, where he made his home for the rest of his life.

"When he died, in November, 1895," says Mr. Heywood, "he was living in the old brown frame-house at Newton Center, Massachusetts, which had been his home for over fifty years. It stood back from the street, on the brow of a hill sloping gently to a valley on the north. Pine trees were in the front and rear, and the sun, from his rising to his setting, smiled upon that abode of simple greatness. The house was faded and worn by wind and weather, and was in perfect harmony with its surroundings—the brown grass sod that peeped from under the snow, the dull-colored, leafless elms, and the gray, worn stone steps leading up from the street.

"An air of gentle refinement pervaded the interior, and every room spoke of its inmate. But perhaps the library was best loved of all by Dr. Smith, for here it was that his work went on. Here, beside a sunny bay window, stood his work table, and his high-backed, old-fashioned chair, with black, rounded arms. All about the room were ranged his bookcases, and an old, tall clock marked the flight of time that was so kind to the old man. His figure was short, his shoulders slightly bowed, and around his full, ruddy face, that beamed with kindness, was a fringe of white hair and beard."

Dr. Smith resigned his pastorate of the Newton church in 1854, and became editorial secretary of the American Baptist Missionary Union. In 1875 he went abroad for the first time, and spent a year in European travel. Five years later he went to India and the Burmese empire. During his travels he visited Christian missionary stations in France, Spain, Italy, Austria, Turkey, Greece, Sweden, Denmark, Burmah, India, and Ceylon.

The latter years of his life were devoted almost entirely to literary work. He wrote numerous poems which were published in magazines and newspapers, but never collected in book form. His hymns, numbering over one hundred, are sung by various Christian denominations. "The Morning Light is Breaking" is a popular favorite. Among his other published works are "Missionary Sketches," "Rambles in Mission Fields," a "History of Newton," and a "Life of Rev. Joseph Grafton." Besides his original hymns, he translated many from other languages, and wrote numerous magazine articles and sketches during his long and busy life.

Dr. Smith's vitality and enthusiasm remained with him to the last. A great-grandfather when he died in his eighty-seventh year, he was an inspiration to the younger generations growing up around him. He was at work almost to the moment of his death, and still actively planning for the future.

His great national hymn, if he had left nothing else, will keep his memory green forever in the hearts of his countrymen. It is even more popular to-day, after seventy-one years have elapsed, than it was when first sung in Park Street Church by the Sunday-school children of Boston. Its patriotic ring, rather than its literary merit, renders it sweet to the ear of every American. Wherever it is sung, the feeble treble of age will join as enthusiastically as the joyous note of youth in rendering the inspiring strains of

AMERICA

My country, 'tis of thee,
Sweet land of liberty,
Of thee I sing,
Land where my fathers died,
Land of the pilgrim's pride,
From every mountain side,
Let freedom ring.

My native country, thee,
Land of the noble, free,
Thy name I love;
I love thy rocks and rills,

Thy woods and templed hills,—
My heart with rapture thrills,
Like that above.

Let music swell the breeze,
And ring from all the trees
Sweet freedom's song;
Let mortal tongues awake,
Let all that breathe partake,
Let rocks their silence break,
The sound prolong.

Our fathers' God, to Thee,
Author of Liberty,
To Thee we sing;
Long may our land be bright
With freedom's holy light,—
Protect us by thy might,
Great God, our King.

III. THE BATTLE HYMN OF THE REPUBLIC

"No single influence," says United States Senator George F. Hoar of Massachusetts, "has had so much to do with shaping the destiny of a nation—as nothing more surely expresses national character—than what is known as the national anthem."

There is some difference of opinion as to which of our patriotic hymns or songs is distinctively the national anthem of America. Senator Hoar seems to have made up his mind in favor of "The Battle Hymn of the Republic." Writing of its author, Julia Ward Howe, in 1903, he said: "We waited eighty years for our American national anthem. At last God inspired an illustrious and noble woman to utter in undying verse the thought which we hope is forever to animate the soldier of the republic:—

"'In the beauty of the lilies Christ was born across the sea
With a glory in His bosom that transfigures you and me;
As He died to make men holy, let us die to make men free,
While God is marching on.'"

Mrs. Julia Ward Howe is as widely known for her learning and literary and poetic achievements as she is for her work as a philanthropist and reformer.

She was born in New York City, in a stately mansion near the Bowling Green, on May 27, 1819. From her birth she was fortunate in possessing the advantages that wealth and high social position bestow. Her father, Samuel Ward, the descendant of an old colonial family, was a member of a leading banking firm of New York. Her mother, Julia Cutter Ward, was a most charming and accomplished woman. She died very young, however, while her little daughter Julia was still a child. Mr. Ward was a man of advanced ideas, and was determined that his daughters should have, as far as possible, the same educational advantages as his sons.

Of course, in those early days there were no separate colleges for women, and they would not be admitted to men's colleges. It was impossible for Mr. Ward to overcome these difficulties wholly, but he did the next best thing he could for his girls. He engaged as their tutor the learned Dr. Joseph Green Cogswell, and instructed him to put them through the full curriculum of Harvard College.

On her entrance into society the "little Miss Ward," as Julia had been called from her childhood, at once became a leader of the cultured and fashionable circle in which she moved. In her father's home she met the most distinguished American men of letters of that time. The liberal education which she had received made the young girl feel perfectly at her ease in such society. In addition to other accomplishments, she was mistress of several ancient and modern languages, and a musical amateur of great promise.

In 1843 Miss Ward was married to Dr. Samuel G. Howe, director of the Institute for the Blind in South Boston, Massachusetts. Immediately after their marriage Dr. and Mrs. Howe went to Europe, where they traveled for some time. The home which they established in Boston on their return became a center for the refined and literary society of Boston and its environment. Mrs. Howe's grace, learning, and accomplishments made her a charming hostess and fit mistress of such a home.

Her literary talent was developed at a very early age. One of her friends has humorously said that "Mrs. Howe wrote leading articles from her cradle." However this may be, it is undoubtedly true that at seventeen she contributed valuable articles to a leading New York magazine. In 1854 she published her first volume of poems, "Passion Flowers." Other volumes, including collections of her later poems, books of travel, and a biography of Margaret Fuller, were afterward published. For more than half a century she has been a constant contributor to the leading magazines of the country.

Since 1869 Mrs. Howe has been a leader in the movement for woman's suffrage, and both by lecturing and writing has supported every effort put forth for the educational and general advancement of her sex.

Although in her eightieth year when the writer conversed with her a few years ago, Mrs. Howe was then full of youthful enthusiasm, and her interest in the great movements of the world was as keen as ever. Age had in no way lessened her intellectual vigor. Surrounded by her children and grandchildren, and one great-grandchild, she recently celebrated her eighty-fourth birthday.

The story of "The Battle Hymn of the Republic" has been left to the last, not because it is the least important, but, on the contrary, because it is one of the most important works of her life. Certain it is that the "Battle Hymn" will live and thrill the hearts of Americans centuries after its author has passed on to the other life.

The hymn was written in Washington, in November, 1861, the first year of our Civil War. Dr. and Mrs. Howe were visiting friends in that city. During their stay, they went one day with a party to see a review of Union troops. The review, however, was interrupted by a movement of the Confederate forces which were besieging the city. On their return, the carriage in which Mrs. Howe and her friends were seated was surrounded by soldiers. Stirred by the scene and the occasion, she began to sing "John Brown," to the delight of the soldiers, who heartily joined in the refrain.

At the close of the song Mrs. Howe expressed to her friends the strong desire she felt to write some words which might be sung to this stirring tune. But she added that she feared she would never be able to do so.

"That night," says her daughter, Maude Howe Eliot, "she went to sleep full of thoughts of battle, and awoke before dawn the next morning to find the desired verses immediately present to her mind. She sprang from her bed, and in the dim gray light found a pen and paper, whereon she wrote, scarcely seeing them, the lines of the poem. Returning to her couch, she was soon asleep, but not until she had said to herself, 'I like this better than anything I have ever written before.'"

THE BATTLE HYMN OF THE REPUBLIC

Mine eyes have seen the glory of the coming of the Lord:
He is trampling out the vintage where the grapes of wrath are stored;
He hath loosed the fateful lightning of His terrible swift sword:
His truth is marching on.

I have seen Him in the watch fires of a hundred circling camps;
They have builded Him an altar in the evening dews and damps;
I can read His righteous sentence by the dim and flaring lamps;
His day is marching on.

I have read a fiery gospel, writ in burnished rows of steel:
"As ye deal with my contemners, so with you my grace shall deal;
Let the Hero born of woman crush the serpent with his heel,
Since God is marching on."

He has sounded forth the trumpet that shall never call retreat;
He is sifting out the hearts of men before His judgment seat:
Oh! be swift, my soul, to answer Him! be jubilant, my feet!
Our God is marching on.

In the beauty of the lilies Christ was born across the sea,
With a glory in His bosom that transfigures you and me:
As he died to make men holy, let us die to make men free,
While God is marching on.

***

TRAINING FOR GREATNESS

GLIMPSES OF ABRAHAM LINCOLN'S BOYHOOD

In pronouncing a eulogy on Henry Clay, Lincoln said: "His example teaches us that one can scarcely be so poor but that, if he will, he can acquire sufficient education to get through the world respectably."

Endowed as he was with all the qualities that make a man truly great, Lincoln's own life teaches above all other things the lesson he drew from that of Henry Clay. Is there in all the length and breadth of the United States to-day a boy so poor as to envy Abraham Lincoln the chances of his boyhood? The story of his life has been told so often that nothing new can be said about him. Yet every fresh reading of the story fills the reader anew with wonder and admiration at what was accomplished by the poor backwoods boy.

Let your mind separate itself from all the marvels of the twentieth century. Think of a time when railroads and telegraph wires, telephones, great ocean steamers, lighting by gas and electricity, daily newspapers (except in a few centers), great circulating libraries, and the hundreds of conveniences which are necessities to the people of to-day, were unknown. Even the very rich at the beginning of the nineteenth century could not buy the advantages that are free to the poorest boy at the beginning of the twentieth century. When Lincoln was a boy, thorns were used for pins; cork covered with cloth or bits of bone served as buttons; crusts of rye bread were used by the poor as substitutes for coffee, and dried leaves of certain herbs for tea.

Abraham Lincoln was born on February 12, 1809, in a log cabin in Hardin County, now La Rue County, Kentucky. His father, Thomas Lincoln, was not remarkable either for thrift or industry. He was tall, well built, and muscular, expert with his rifle, and a noted hunter, but he did not possess the qualities necessary to make a successful pioneer farmer. The character of the mother of Abraham, may best be gathered from his own words: "All that I am or hope to be," he said when president of the United States, "I owe to my angel mother. Blessings on her memory!"

It was at her knee he learned his first lessons from the Bible. With his sister Sarah, a girl two years his senior, he listened with wonder and delight to the Bible stories, fairy tales, and legends with which the gentle mother entertained and instructed them when the labors of the day were done.

When Abraham was about four years old, the family moved from the farm on Nolin Creek to another about fifteen miles distant. There the first great event in his life took place. He went to school. Primitive as was the log-cabin schoolhouse, and elementary as were the acquirements of his first schoolmaster, it was a wonderful experience for the boy, and one that he never forgot.

In 1816 Thomas Lincoln again decided to make a change. He was enticed by stories that came to him from Indiana to try his fortunes there. So, once more the little family "pulled up stakes" and moved on to the place selected by the father in Spencer County, about a mile and a half from Gentryville. It was a long, toilsome journey through the forest, from the old home in Kentucky to the new one in Indiana. In some places they had to clear their way through the tangled thickets as they journeyed along. The stock of provisions they carried with them was supplemented by game snared or shot in the forest and fish caught in the river. These they cooked over the wood fire, kindled by means of tinder and flint. The interlaced branches of trees and the sky made the roof of their bedchamber by night, and pine twigs their bed.

When the travelers arrived at their destination, there was no time for rest after their journey. Some sort of shelter had to be provided at once for their accommodation. They hastily put up a "half-faced camp"—a sort of rude tent, with an opening on one side. The framework of the tent was of upright posts, crossed by thin slabs, cut from the trees they felled. The open side, or entrance, was covered with "pelts," or half-dressed skins of wild animals. There was no ruder dwelling in the wilds of Indiana, and no poorer family among the settlers than the new adventurers from Kentucky. They were reduced to the most primitive makeshifts in order to eke out a living. There was no lack of food, however, for the woods were full of game of all kinds, both feathered and furred, and the streams and rivers abounded with fish. But the home lacked everything in the way of comfort or convenience.

Abraham, who was then in his eighth year, has been described as a tall, ungainly, fast-growing, long-legged lad, clad in the garb of the frontier. This consisted of a shirt of linsey-woolsey, a coarse homespun material made of linen and wool, a pair of home-made moccasins, deerskin leggings or breeches, and a hunting shirt of the same material. This costume was completed by a coonskin cap, the tail of the animal being left to hang down the wearer's back as an ornament.

This sturdy lad, who was born to a life of unremitting toil, was already doing a man's work. From the time he was four years old, away back on the Kentucky farm, he had contributed his share to the family labors. Picking berries, dropping seeds, and doing other simple tasks suited to his strength, he had thus early begun his apprenticeship to toil. In putting up the "half-faced" camp, he was his father's principal helper. Afterward, when they built a more, substantial cabin to take the place of the camp, he learned to handle an ax, a maul, and a wedge. He helped to fell trees, fashion logs, split rails, and do other important work in building the one-roomed cabin, which was to be the permanent home of the family. He assisted also in making the rough tables and chairs and the one rude bedstead or bed frame which constituted the principal furniture of the cabin. In his childhood Abraham did not enjoy the luxury of sleeping on a bedstead. His bed was simply a heap of dry leaves, which occupied a corner of the loft over the cabin. He climbed to it every night by a stepladder, or rather a number of pegs driven into the wall.

Rough and poor and full of hardship as his life was, Lincoln was by no means a sad or unhappy boy. On the contrary, he was full of fun and boyish pranks. His life in the open air, the vigorous exercise of every muscle which necessity forced upon him, the tonic of the forests which he breathed from his infancy, his interest in every living and growing thing about him,—all helped to make him unusually strong, healthy, buoyant, and rich in animal spirits.

The first great sorrow of his life came to him in the death of his dearly loved mother in 1818. The boy mourned for her as few children mourn even for the most loving parent. Day after day he went from the home made desolate by her death to weep on her grave under the near-by trees.

There were no churches in the Indiana wilderness, and the visits of wandering ministers of religion to the scattered settlements were few and far between. Little Abraham was grieved that no funeral service had been held over his dead mother. He felt that it was in some sense a lack of respect to her. He thought a great deal about the matter, and finally wrote a letter to a minister named Elkins, whom the family had known in Kentucky. Several months after the receipt of the letter Parson Elkins came to Indiana. On the Sabbath morning after his arrival, in the presence of friends who had come long distances to assist, he read the funeral service over the grave of Mrs. Lincoln. He also spoke in touching words of the tender Christian mother who lay buried there. This simple service greatly comforted the heart of the lonely boy.

Some time after Thomas Lincoln brought a new mother to his children from Kentucky. This was Mrs. Sally Bush Johnston, a young widow, who had been a girlhood friend of Nancy Hanks. She had three children,—John, Sarah, and Matilda Johnston,—who accompanied her to Indiana. The second Mrs. Lincoln brought a stock of household goods and furniture with her from Kentucky, and with the help of these made so many improvements in the rude log cabin that her stepchildren regarded her as a sort of magician or wonder worker. She was a good mother to them, intelligent, kind, and loving.

He was ten years old at this time, and had been to school but little. Indeed, he says himself that he only went to school "by littles," and that all his schooling "did not amount to more than a year." But he had learned to read when he was a mere baby at his mother's knee; and to a boy who loved knowledge as he did, this furnished the key to a broad education. His love of reading amounted to a passion. The books he had access to when a boy were very few; but they were good ones, and he knew them literally from cover to cover. They were the Bible, "Robinson Crusoe," "Pilgrim's Progress," a "History of the United States," and Weems's "Life of Washington." Some of these were borrowed, among them the "Life of Washington," of which Abraham afterward became the happy owner. The story of how he became its owner has often been told.

The book had been loaned to him by a neighbor, a well-to-do farmer named Crawford. After reading from it late into the night by the light of pine knots, Abraham carried it to his bedroom in the loft. He placed it in a crack between the logs over his bed of dry leaves, so that he could reach to it as soon as the first streaks of dawn penetrated through the chinks in the log cabin. Unfortunately, it rained heavily during the night, and when he took down the precious volume in the morning, he found it badly damaged, all soddened and stained by the rain. He was much distressed, and hurried to the owner of the book as soon as possible to explain the mishap.

"I'm real sorry, Mr. Crawford," he said, in concluding his explanation, "and want to fix it up with you somehow, if you can tell me any way, for I ain't got the money to pay for it with."

"Well," said Mr. Crawford, "being as it's you, Abe, I won't be hard on you. Come over and shuck corn three days, and the book's yours."

The boy was delighted with the result of what at first had seemed a great misfortune. Verily, his sorrow was turned into joy. What! Shuck corn only three days and become owner of the book that told all about his greatest hero! What an unexpected piece of good fortune!

Lincoln's reading had revealed to him a world beyond his home in the wilderness. Slowly it dawned upon him that one day he might find his place in that great world, and he resolved to prepare himself with all his might for whatever the future might hold.

"I don't intend to delve, grub, shuck corn, split rails, and the like always," he told Mrs. Crawford after he had finished reading the "Life of Washington." "I'm going to fit myself for a profession."

"Why, what do you want to be now?" asked Mrs. Crawford, in surprise. "Oh, I'll be president," said the boy, with a smile.

"You'd make a pretty president, with all your tricks and jokes, now wouldn't you?" said Mrs. Crawford.

"Oh, I'll study and get ready," was the reply, "and then maybe the chance will come."

If the life of George Washington, who had all the advantages of culture and training that his time afforded, was an inspiration to Lincoln, the poor hard-working backwoods boy, what should the life of Lincoln be to boys of to-day? Here is a further glimpse of the way in which he prepared himself to be president of the United States. The quotation is from Ida M. Tarbell's "Life of Lincoln."

"Every lull in his daily labor he used for reading, rarely going to his work without a book. When plowing or cultivating the rough fields of Spencer County, he found frequently a half hour for reading, for at the end of every long row the horse was allowed to rest, and Lincoln had his book out and was perched on stump or fence, almost as soon as the plow had come to a standstill. One of the few people left in Gentryville who still remembers Lincoln, Captain John Lamar, tells to this day of riding to mill with his father, and seeing, as they drove along, a boy sitting on the top rail of an old-fashioned, stake-and-rider worm fence, reading so intently that he did not notice their approach. His father, turning to him, said: 'John, look at that boy yonder, and mark my words, he will make a smart man out of himself. I may not see it, but you'll see if my words don't come true.' 'That boy was Abraham Lincoln,' adds Mr. Lamar, impressively."

Lincoln's father was illiterate, and had no sympathy with his son's efforts to educate himself. Fortunately for him, however, his stepmother helped and encouraged him in every way possible. Shortly before her death she said to a biographer of Lincoln: "I induced my husband to permit Abe to read and study at home, as well as at school. At first he was not easily reconciled to it, but finally he too seemed willing to encourage him to a certain extent. Abe was a dutiful son to me always, and we took particular care when he was reading not to disturb him,—would let him read on and on till he quit of his own accord."

Lincoln fully appreciated his stepmother's sympathy and love for him, and returned them in equal measure. It added greatly to his enjoyment of his reading and studies to have some one to whom he could talk about them, and in after life he always gratefully remembered what his second mother did for him in those early days of toil and effort.

If there was a book to be borrowed anywhere in his neighborhood, he was sure to hear about it and borrow it if possible. He said himself that he "read through every book he had ever heard of in that county for a circuit of fifty miles."

And how he read! Boys who have books and magazines and papers in abundance in their homes, besides having thousands of volumes to choose from in great city libraries, can have no idea of what a book meant to this boy in the wilderness. He devoured every one that came into his hands as a man famishing from hunger devours a crust of bread. He read and re-read it until he had made the contents his own.

"From everything he read," says Miss Tarbell, "he made long extracts, with his turkey-buzzard pen and brier-root ink. When he had no paper he would write on a board, and thus preserve his selections until he secured a copybook. The wooden fire shovel was his usual slate, and on its back he ciphered with a charred stick, shaving it off when it had become too grimy for use. The logs and boards in his vicinity he covered with his figures and quotations. By night he read and worked as long as there was light, and he kept a book in the crack of the logs in his loft to have it at hand at peep of day. When acting as ferryman on the Ohio in his nineteenth year, anxious, no doubt, to get through the books of the house where he boarded before he left the place, he read every night until midnight."

His stepmother said: "He read everything he could lay his hands on, and when he came across a passage that struck him, he would write it down on boards if he had no paper, and keep it by him until he could get paper. Then he would copy it, look at it, commit it to memory, and repeat it."

His thoroughness in mastering everything he undertook to study was a habit acquired in childhood. How he acquired this habit he tells himself. "Among my earliest recollections I remember how, when a mere child," he says, "I used to get irritated when anybody talked to me in a way I could not understand. I do not think I ever got angry at anything else in my life; but that always disturbed my temper, and has ever since. I can remember going to my little bedroom, after hearing the neighbors talk of an evening with my father, and spending no small part of the night walking up and down and trying to make out what was the exact meaning of some of their—to me—dark sayings.

"I could not sleep, although I tried to, when I got on such a hunt for an idea until I had caught it; and when I thought I had got it, I was not satisfied until I had repeated it over and over; until I had put it in language plain enough, as I thought, for any boy I knew to comprehend. This was a kind of passion with me, and it has stuck by me; for I am never easy now when I am handling a thought, till I have bounded it north and bounded it south and bounded it east and bounded it west."

With all his hard study, reading, and thinking, Lincoln was not a bookworm, nor a dull companion to the humble, unschooled people among whom his youth was spent. On the contrary, although he was looked up to as one whose acquirements in "book learning" had raised him far above every one in his neighborhood, he was the most popular youth in all the country round. No "husking bee," or "house raising" or merry-making of any kind was complete if Abraham was not present. He was witty, ready of speech, a good story-teller, and had stored his memory with a fund of humorous anecdotes, which he always used to good purpose and with great effect. He had committed to memory, and could recite all the poetry in the various school readers used at that time in the log-cabin schoolhouse. He could make rhymes himself, and even make impromptu speeches that excited the admiration of his hearers. He was the best wrestler, jumper, runner, and the strongest of all his young companions. Even when a mere youth he could lift as much as three full-grown men; and, "if you heard him fellin' trees in a clearin'," said his cousin, Dennis Hanks, "you would say there was three men at work by the way the trees fell. His ax would flash and bite into a sugar tree or sycamore, and down it would come."

His kindness and tenderness of heart were as great as his strength and agility. He loved all God's creatures, and cruelty to any of them always aroused his indignation. Only once did he ever attempt to kill any of the game in the woods, which the family considered necessary for their subsistence. He refers to this occasion in an autobiography, written by him in the third person, in the year 1860.

"A few days before the completion of his eighth year," he says, "in the absence of his father, a flock of wild turkeys approached the new log cabin; and Abraham, with a rifle gun, standing inside, shot through a crack and killed one of them. He has never since pulled the trigger on any larger game."

Any suffering thing, whether it was animal, man, woman, or child, was sure of his sympathy and aid. Although he never touched intoxicating drinks himself, he pitied those who lost manhood by their use. One night on his way home from a husking bee or house raising, he found an unfortunate man lying on the roadside overcome with drink. If the man were allowed to remain there, he would freeze to death. Lincoln raised him from the ground and carried him a long distance to the nearest house, where he remained with him during the night. The man was his firm friend ever after.

Women admired him for his courtesy and rough gallantry, as well as for his strength and kindness of heart; and he, in his turn, reverenced women, as every noble, strong man does. This big, bony, tall, awkward young fellow, who at eighteen measured six feet four, was as ready to care for a baby in the absence of its mother as he was to tell a good story or to fell a tree. Was it any wonder that he was popular with all kinds of people?

His stepmother says of him: "Abe was a good boy, and I can say what scarcely one woman—a mother—can say in a thousand; Abe never gave me a cross word or look, and never refused in fact or appearance to do anything I requested him. I never gave him a cross word in all my life. His mind and mine—what little I had—seemed to run together. He was here after he was elected president. He was a dutiful son to me always. I think he loved me truly. I had a son, John, who was raised with Abe. Both were good boys; but I must say, both now being dead, that Abe was the best boy I ever saw or expect to see."

Wherever he went, or whatever he did, he studied men and things, and gathered knowledge as much by observation as from books and whatever news-papers or other publications he could get hold of. He used to go regularly to the leading store in Gentryville, to read a Louisville paper, taken by the proprietor of the store, Mr. Jones. He discussed its contents, and exchanged views with the farmers who made the store their place of meeting. His love of oratory was great. When the courts were in session in Boonville, a town fifteen miles distant from his home, whenever he could spare a day, he used to walk there in the morning and back at night, to hear the lawyers argue cases and make speeches. By this time Abraham himself could make an impromptu speech on any subject with which he was at all familiar, good enough to win the applause of the Indiana farmers.

So, his boyhood days, rough, hard-working days, but not devoid of fun and recreation, passed. Abraham did not love work any more than other country boys of his age, but he never shirked his tasks. Whether it was plowing, splitting rails, felling trees, doing chores, reaping, threshing, or any of the multitude of things to be done on a farm, the work was always well done. Sometimes, to make a diversion, when he was working as a "hired hand," he would stop to tell some of his funny stories, or to make a stump speech before his fellow-workers, who would all crowd round him to listen; but he would more than make up for the time thus spent by the increased energy with which he afterward worked. Doubtless the other laborers, too, were refreshed and stimulated to greater effort by the recreation he afforded them and the inspiration of his example.

Thomas Lincoln had learned carpentry and cabinet making in his youth, and taught the rudiments of these trades to his son; so that in addition to his skill and efficiency in all the work that falls to the lot of a pioneer backwoods farmer, Abraham added the accomplishment of being a fairly good carpenter. He worked at these trades with his father whenever the opportunity offered. When he was not working for his family, he was hired out to the neighboring farmers. His highest wage was twenty-five cents a day, which he always handed over to his father.

Lincoln got his first glimpse of the world beyond Indiana when he worked for several months as a ferryman and boatman on the Ohio River, at Anderson Creek. He saw the steamers and vessels of all kinds sailing up and down the Ohio, laden with produce and merchandise, on their way to and from western and southern towns. He came in contact with different kinds of people from different states, and thus his views of the world and its people became a little more extended, and his longing to be somebody and to do something worth while in the world waxed stronger daily.

His work as a ferryman showed him that there were other ways of making a little money than by hiring out to the neighbors at twenty-five cents a day. He resolved to take some of the farm produce to New Orleans and sell it there. This project led to the unexpected earning of a dollar, which added strength to his purpose to prepare himself to take the part of a man in the world outside of Indiana. Let him tell in his own words, as he related the story to Mr. Seward years afterward, how he earned the dollar:—

"Seward," he said, "did you ever hear how I earned my first dollar?"

"No," said Mr. Seward.

"Well," replied he, "I was about eighteen years of age, and belonged, as you know, to what they call down south the 'scrubs'; people who do not own land and slaves are nobodies there; but we had succeeded in raising, chiefly by my labor, sufficient produce, as I thought, to justify me in taking it down the river to sell. After much persuasion I had got the consent of my mother to go, and had constructed a flatboat large enough to take the few barrels of things we had gathered to New Orleans. A steamer was going down the river. We have, you know, no wharves on the western streams, and the custom was, if passengers were at any of the landings, they were to go out in a boat, the steamer stopping and taking them on board. I was contemplating my new boat, and wondering whether I could make it stronger or improve it in any part, when two men with trunks came down to the shore in carriages, and looking at the different boats singled out mine, and asked, 'Who owns this?' I answered modestly, 'I do.' 'Will you,' said one of them, 'take us and our trunks to the steamer?' 'Certainly,' said I. I was very glad to have the chance of earning something, and supposed that each of them would give me a couple of bits. The trunks were put in my boat, the passengers seated themselves on them, and I sculled them out to the steamer. They got on board, and I lifted the trunks and put them on the deck. The steamer was about to put on steam again, when I called out, 'You have forgotten to pay me.' Each of them took from his pocket a silver half-dollar and threw it on the bottom of my boat. I could scarcely believe my eyes as I picked up the money. You may think it was a very little thing, and in these days it seems to me like a trifle, but it was a most important incident in my life. I could scarcely credit that I, the poor boy, had earned a dollar in less than a day; that by honest work I had earned a dollar. I was a more hopeful and thoughtful boy from that time."

In March, 1828, Lincoln was employed by one of the leading men of Gentryville to take a load of produce down the Mississippi River to New Orleans. For this service he was paid eight dollars a month and his rations.

This visit to New Orleans was a great event in his life. It showed him the life of a busy cosmopolitan city, which was a perfect wonderland to him. Everything he saw aroused his astonishment and interest, and served to educate him for the larger life on which he was to enter later.

The next important event in the history of the Lincoln family was their removal from Indiana to Illinois in 1830. The farm in Indiana had not prospered as they hoped it would,—hence the removal to new ground in Illinois. Abraham drove the team of oxen which carried their household goods from the old home to their new abiding place near Decatur, in Macon County, Illinois. Driving over the muddy, ill-made roads with a heavily laden team was hard and slow work, and the journey occupied a fortnight. When they arrived at their destination, Lincoln again helped to build a log cabin for the family home. With his stepbrother he also, as he said himself, "made sufficient of rails to fence ten acres of ground, and raised a crop of sown corn upon it the same year."

In that same year, 1830, he reached his majority. It was time for him to be about his own business. He had worked patiently and cheerfully since he was able to hold an ax in his hands for his own and the family's maintenance. They could now get along without him, and he felt that the time had come for him to develop himself for larger duties.

He left the log cabin, penniless, without even a good suit of clothes. The first work he did when he became his own master was to supply this latter deficiency. For a certain Mrs. Millet he "split four hundred rails for every yard of brown jeans, dyed with white walnut bark, necessary to make a pair of trousers."

For nearly a year he continued to work as a rail splitter and farm "hand." Then he was hired by a Mr. Denton Offut to take a flatboat loaded with goods from Sangamon town to New Orleans. So well pleased was Mr. Offut with the way in which Lincoln executed his commission that on his return he engaged him to take charge of a mill and store at New Salem.

There, as in every other place in which he had resided, he became the popular favorite. His kindness of heart, his good humor, his skill as a story teller, his strength, his courtesy, manliness, and honesty were such as to win all hearts. He would allow no man to use profane language before women. A boorish fellow who insisted on doing so in the store on one occasion, in spite of Lincoln's protests, found this out to his cost. Lincoln had politely requested him not to use such language before ladies, but the man persisted in doing so. When the women left the store, he became violently angry and began to abuse Lincoln. He wanted to pick a quarrel with him. Seeing this Lincoln said, "Well, if you must be whipped, I suppose I may as well whip you as any other man," and taking the man out of the store he gave him a well-merited chastisement. Strange to say, he became Lincoln's friend after this, and remained so to the end of his life.

His scrupulous honesty won for him in the New Salem community the title of "Honest Abe," a title which is still affectionately applied to him. On one occasion, having by mistake overcharged a customer six and a quarter cents, he walked three miles after the store was closed in order to restore the customer's money. At another time, in weighing tea for a woman, he used a quarter-pound instead of a half-pound weight. When he went to use the scales again, he discovered his mistake, and promptly walked a long distance to deliver the remainder of the tea.

Lincoln's determination to improve himself continued to be the leading object of his life. He said once to his fellow-clerk in the store, "I have talked with great men, and I do not see how they differ from others." His observation had taught him that the great difference in men's positions was not due so much to one having more talents or being more highly gifted than another, but rather to the way in which one cultivated his talent or talents and another neglected his.

Up to this time he had not made a study of grammar, but he realized that if he were to speak in public he must learn to speak grammatically. He had no grammar, and did not know where to get one. In this dilemma he consulted the schoolmaster of New Salem, who told him where and from whom he could borrow a copy of Kirkham's Grammar. The place named was six miles from New Salem. But that was nothing to a youth so hungry for an education as Lincoln. He immediately started for the residence of the fortunate people who owned a copy of Kirkham's Grammar. The book was loaned to him without hesitation. In a short time its contents were mastered, the student studying at night by the light of shavings burned in the village cooper's shop. "Well," said Lincoln to Greene, his fellow-clerk, when he had turned over the last page of the grammar, "if that's what they call a science, I think I'll go at another." The conquering of one thing after another, the thorough mastery of whatever he undertook to do, made the next thing easier of accomplishment than it would otherwise have been. In order to practice debating he used to walk seven or eight miles to debating clubs. No labor or trouble seemed too great to him if by it he could increase his knowledge or add to his acquirements. No matter how hard or exhausting his work, whether it was rail splitting, plowing, lumbering, boating, or store keeping, he studied and read every spare minute, and often until late at night.

But this sketch has already exceeded the limits of Lincoln's boyhood, for he had reached his twenty-second year while in the store in New Salem. How he was made captain of a company raised to fight against the Indians, how he kept store for himself, learned surveying, was elected a member of the Illinois legislature, studied law, and was admitted to the bar in Springfield, and how he finally became president of the United States,—all this belongs to a later chapter of his life.

Lincoln's rise from the poorest of log cabins to the White House, to be president of the greatest republic in the world, is one of the most inspiring stories in American biography. Yet he was not a genius, unless a determination to make the most of one's self and to persist in spite of all hardships, discouragements, and hindrances, be genius. He made himself what he was—one of the noblest, greatest, and best of men—by sheer dint of hard work and the cultivation of the talents that had been given him. No fortunate chances, no influential friends, no rare opportunities played a part in his life. Alone and unaided he made, by the grace of God, the great career which will forever challenge the admiration of mankind.

***

THE MARBLE WAITETH

THE STATUE

The marble waits, immaculate and rude;
    Beside it stands the sculptor, lost in dreams.
    With vague, chaotic forms his vision teems.
Fair shapes pursue him, only to elude
And mock his eager fancy. Lines of grace
    And heavenly beauty vanish, and, behold!
    Out through the Parian luster, pure and cold,
Glares the wild horror of a devil's face.

The clay is ready for the modeling.
    The marble waits: how beautiful, how pure,
    That gleaming substance, and it shall endure,
When dynasty and empire, throne and king
Have crumbled back to dust. Well may you pause,
    Oh, sculptor-artist! and, before that mute,
    Unshapen surface, stand irresolute!
Awful, indeed, are art's unchanging laws.

The thing you fashion out of senseless clay,
    Transformed to marble, shall outlive your fame;
    And, when no more is known your race, or name,
Men shall be moved by what you mold to-day.
We all are sculptors. By each act and thought,
    We form the model. Time, the artisan,
    Stands, with his chisel, fashioning the Man,
And stroke by stroke the masterpiece is wrought.

Angel or demon? Choose, and do not err!
    For time but follows as you shape the mold,
    And finishes in marble, stern and cold,
That statue of the soul, the character.

By wordless blessing, or by silent curse,
By act and motive,—so do you define
The image which time copies, line by line,
For the great gallery of the Universe.

ELLA WHEELER WILCOX.

At the gateway of a new year, emerging from the gay carelessness of childhood, stand troops of buoyant, eager-eyed youths and maidens, gazing down the vista of the future with glad expectancy.

Fancy spreads upon her canvas radiant pictures of the joys and triumphs which await them in the unborn years. In their unclouded springtime there is no place for the specters of doubt and fear which too often overshadow the autumn of life.

In this formative period, the soul is unsoiled by warfare with the world. It lies, like a block of pure, uncut Parian marble, ready to be fashioned into—what?

Its possibilities are limitless. You are the sculptor. An unseen hand places in yours the mallet and the chisel, and a voice whispers: "The marble waiteth. What will you do with it?"

In this same block the angel and the demon lie sleeping. Which will you call into life? Blows of some sort you must strike. The marble cannot be left uncut. From its crudity some shape must be evolved. Shall it be one of beauty, or of deformity; an angel, or a devil? Will you shape it into a statue of beauty which will enchant the world, or will you call out a hideous image which will demoralize every beholder?

What are your ideals, as you stand facing the dawn of this new year with the promise and responsibility of the new life on which you have entered, awaiting you? Upon them depends the form which the rough block shall take. Every stroke of the chisel is guided by the ideal behind the blow.

Look at this easy-going, pleasure-loving youth who takes up the mallet and smites the chisel with careless, thoughtless blows. His mind is filled with images of low, sensual pleasures; the passing enjoyment of the hour is everything to him; his work, the future, nothing. He carries in his heart, perhaps, the bestial motto of the glutton, "Eat, drink, and be merry, for to-morrow we die;" or the flippant maxim of the gay worldling, "A short life and a merry one; the foam of the chalice for me;" forgetting that beneath the foam are the bitter dregs, which, be he ever so unwilling, he must swallow, not to-day, nor yet to-morrow,—perhaps not this year nor next; but sometime, as surely as the reaping follows the sowing, will the bitter draught follow the foaming glass of unlawful pleasure.

As the years go by, and youth merges into manhood, the sculptor's hand becomes more unsteady. One false blow follows another in rapid succession. The formless marble takes on distorted outlines. Its whiteness has long since become spotted. The sculptor, with blurred vision and shattered nerves, still strikes with aimless hand, carving deep gashes, adding a crooked line here, another there, soiling and marring until no trace of the virgin purity of the block of marble which was given him remains. It has become so grimy, so demoniacally fantastic in its outlines, that the beholder turns from it with a shudder.

Not far off we see another youth at work on a block of marble, similar in every detail to the first. The tools with which he plies his labor differ in no wise from those of the worker we have been following.

The glory of the morning shines upon the marble. Glowing with enthusiasm, the light of a high purpose illuminating his face, the sculptor, with steady hand and eye, begins to work out his ideal. The vision that flits before him is so beautiful that he almost fears the cunning of his hand will be unequal to fashioning it from the rigid mass before him. Patiently he measures each blow of the mallet. With infinite care he chisels each line and curve. Every stroke is true.

Months stretch into years, and still we find the sculptor at work. Time has given greater precision to his touch, and the skill of the youth, strengthened by noble aspirations and right effort, has become positive genius in the man. If he has not attained the ideal that haunted him, he has created a form so beautiful in its clear-cut outlines, so imposing in the majesty of its purity and strength, that the beholder involuntarily bows before it.

THE MARBLE WAITETH. WHAT WILL YOU DO WITH IT?